Helen and Michael

From the Other Side of the Water

all the best

Malcolm

Helen and Michael

all rev best

Malcolm

From the Other Side of the Water

✸

Malcolm S. Mason

Copyright © 2005 by Malcolm S. Mason.

Library of Congress Number: 2003096106
ISBN: Hardcover 1-4134-2832-0
      Softcover 1-4134-2831-2

All rights reserved. No part of this book may be reproduced or transmitted in any form or by any means, electronic or mechanical, including photocopying, recording, or by any information storage and retrieval system, without permission in writing from the copyright owner.

This book was printed in the United States of America.

To order additional copies of this book, contact:
Xlibris Corporation
1-888-795-4274
www.Xlibris.com
Orders@Xlibris.com
21086

Malcolm S. Mason has published many articles and books on contract law, comparative law, brief writing, international law and wartime alien property law, mediation, symbolic logic, federal grant law, statutory drafting.

Most recently in book form:

(With Paul G. Dembling) Essentials of Grant Law Practice (American Law Institute—American Bar Association Committee on Continuing Professional Education, 1991)

From the Other Side of the Water:

>Starting
>
>Learning
>
>Living

In preparation:

>From the Other Side of the Water:
>
>>Laughing
>>
>>Fearing
>>
>>Singing
>>
>>Loving
>>
>>Ending

Some errata to the first two chapters of this book, From the Other Side of the Water, Starting, Learning. (I am sure this list of errata cannot be complete because, with age, it has become very difficult for me to read. I have glaucoma, macular degeneration, a retinal problem, and cataract.)

p. 13, bottom line " should be '

p. 15, l. 24, footnote (°) after child should move right to after him

before p. 167, there should be a title page for chapter Learning

p. 173, l. 3 from bottom, needs a ° (The use of ° instead of numbered footnotes is the result of my misunderstanding Xlibris's instructions.)

p. 174, l. 7, does not need a °

p. 174, l. 2 from bottom, needs a °

p. 183, l. 12, needs a °

p. 190, l. 4, delete the apostrophe

p. 192, l. 13, page by page needs a °

p. 197, l. 4 from the bottom, comma after shadow should be semi-colon

p. 212, l. 5 from bottom, has Italian che twice instead of Spanish que

p. 226, l. 4, or should be on

p. 237, l. 7 from bottom, shcolarship should be scholarship

p.238, l. 9, relies should be rely

p. 240, l. 9, the best teller of these stories should be in italics

p. 242, l. 3 from bottom, 1935 should be 1938

p. 243, l. 5 from bottom, its protections should be the protections

p. 244, notes are in wrong order – the right order is: Williston, Corbin

    Precedents on Both Sides

    Converting the Joint Representation Plan

    No Ideas

    Aristotle

    Reversed the Phenotypes

p.249, notes are in wrong order – the right order is:

    James Joyce

    Goebel, Struggle for the Falkland Islands

Published

A tribute to Jules Goebel

Quinine

Hofstadter, pi-lingiual

Hay Foot – Straw Foot

p. 250, l. 10, Airline should be Aniline

From the Other Side of the Water

Living

III. LIVING

Yoetz (Counselor)
The Guillotine
A Mason gesture
Counselor of God
God Forbid
The Egyptians shall hear it
Shall one man sin?
Unless she had turned from me
Advisor
Counselor or Scrivener
Shipping Archives
Experts
There were two men in a chimney
Hear now
Managing
Aza stobbrich a man
The explosion of the Carib Queen
Stiff-necked
Naïve Intellectualism
De Weg Naar Maastricht, alsdublieft
Myths
Es iz shver tzu zain a yid
Anti-Semitism in Law Practice
Apologia Pro "Vita" Sua
I am not Prince Hamlet
Upper Lower
Chapters of the Fathers
Truth
Truth in the law

Dichtung und Wahrheit
Yiddish faking
Success in practice?
Mammon
Missed Manners
Cognitive Dissonance—Saying No
Charity
Fair Share
Memory
Geography
Why I am not a teacher
Philosophy
Empty Words
Law
History
Lectures
Dictionaries
Labor complaint
Counting
Speaking in tongues
We were slaves
Anarchy
Agenda
Shrimp
Floating
Schadenfreude and Envy
A Profile
Moreh Nebuchim (Guide to the Perplexed)

Verse

My Abominable Autobiography

Irma's Line
Irma's Family Tree
Irma's Family Pictures

LIVING

1/13/95

Yoetz (Counselor)

Among the names for lawyers, there are different shadings of lawyer's work—attorney, advocate, solicitor, barrister, scrivener, counselor. Although I have had a share in many of them, the role I find most congenial is that of counselor.

Paul Dembling[1] and I in our chapter on The Role of the Lawyer[2] have concentrated the advice of many years of law practice both in and out of government. We point out that lawyers are the only group of professionals who are trained to exercise hindsight in advance. Lawyers alone are trained to face the question: what will the action we are taking now look like in hindsight after it is known to be wrong or after a number of facts we do not now know have become known?

On the whole, I work better as a # 2 than as a # 1. Let someone make the go/no-go decisions. I am a good advisor and most comfortable in that role.

When challenged, I generally stand up to responsibilities I would rather not have. In 1948-1952, and again in 1975-1980, I reached a peak in which (I believe) I was an effective decision maker. But I would not want to be President, nor Chief of Staff, nor Attorney General. I could have been an excellent counselor to any of them, or Justice of the Supreme Court, or Judge of a Court of Appeals, but not a judge of a trial court. I don't want Ito's job[3].

I feel certain I would have given Nixon better advice than his Californians did, Carter better advice than his Georgians did, Clinton better advice than his Arkansawns did.

Connected with my preference for an advisory role, is the fact that over the years I have worked perhaps better on the whole with Republican bosses than with Democratic.

At OAP, I got along well with Dallas Townshend, Eisenhower's appointee (although I had also with his Democratic predecessors).

When I worked for Sargent Shriver, I approved his goals and admired his energy and courage, and his willingness to acknowledge error when shown to be wrong. But I was very conscious of what I saw as some of his weaknesses, especially the ease with which he was taken in, as many of us saw it, by plausible advisors who pissed next to him in the Men's room. (This was so well known that female staff members made a *standing* grievance out of it).

A sidelight to this: Drew Pearson falsely published a rumor that Sarge had built a private toilet for himself adjoining his office. Nearly everyone at OEO knew that that was false and Pearson was invited to come in and inspect. He did not come and never retracted. [On the other hand, I have had in government service, particularly three offices at OAP, a private toilet and shower[4] because we occupied commercial space that had been built that way for *private sector* executives.]

When Republicans took over OEO, I did not have to approve their goals, but I could look dispassionately at what the law required them to do and at the means that would achieve their goals if legally permissible. I could give good professional advice, which Don Lowitz, for example, Republican General Counsel in Nixon's time, appreciated highly, after initial resistance.

Frank Carlucci, Republican Director of Operations, after a distinguished Foreign Service career, on my first meeting with him, overrode my advice but, to his great credit in my eyes, later explicitly acknowledged to me and, without telling me so, to others, as I later learned, that he would have done better to have followed it.

Howard Phillips, Nixon's Director of OEO, overrode my advice, but he was under orders from Nixon to do what I advised against. These decisions were reversed and Phillips was removed from office by a Federal District Judge on stated technical grounds but obviously influenced by a strong feeling about his actions.[5]

At HEW, I got along well with John Rhinelander, Republican General Counsel, and Caspar Weinberger, then Secretary, but not with Democrat Califano nor his General Counsel. Again, like Carter and Clinton, Califano brought in with him his own set of advisors some of whom, in my opinion, misled him about issues important to me.

I do not regard this ability to give good technical advice to decision-makers whose goals I may not approve, as a strength. It is a weakness.

The Guillotine

Three men were sentenced to the guillotine, a Nazi, a French Communist, and a Jew.

The Nazi clicked his heels, raised his hand in salute, said Heil Hitler, and laid his head on the block. The knife came down, shuddered to a halt a half inch from his neck. The Commandant directed that, after such an ordeal, the prisoner should not be executed again, and he was released.

The Frenchman raised his fist, cried Vive la Révolution, and laid his head on the block. Again the knife stopped just short. Again, he was released.

The Jew stepped up and said, Well, I can tell you why your guillotine isn't working. See, there is a twist in the cord right there . . .

Jewish humor tradition takes for granted this imperative need to enlighten others.

When you tell a joke to a peasant, he laughs three times: once when you tell him the joke, once when you explain it, once when he gets it.

When you tell a joke to the landowner, he laughs twice: once when you tell him the joke, once when you explain it. Get it? He never gets it.

When you tell a joke to an officer, he laughs once: when you tell him the joke. Explain it? He won't let you explain it. And get it? He never gets it.[6]

When you tell a joke to a Jew, he says, that's an *old* joke, and you don't *tell* it right. Here's how you are *supposed* to tell it . . .

I have been a member of a Yiddish study group. Our principal activity is reading out loud in turn from imperfect photocopies. Most of us are old. Our hearing is poor. Our sight is poor. The letters are often hard to distinguish from one another. But let there be the smallest error—if someone reads (eyn) (no) instead of (un) (and), say—the poorest reader in the group is sure to rap out a magisterial correction. Often four or five will call out the correction. The reader is usually more confused than ever by the cross talk. But the imperative to correct seems to be irresistible.

A Mason gesture

A typical Mason gesture: my sister, my daughter, then perhaps 6, and I, abreast, approached a street corner. The traffic light was in our favor, but as we stepped off the curb, a car jumped against the light across our path. Three sets of arms darted up. Each of us automatically sought to protect the other two.[7]

Counselor of God

Isaiah says (9.5 in the Hebrew text, 9.6 in the Vulgate), Unto us a child is born, unto us a son is given, and his name shall be called Pele yoetz ha el ha gibbor, Wonderful counselor of the mighty God . . .

I punctuate this differently from the standard Christian version that we hear in Handel. I am trying to follow the punctuation of the Masoretic text, but this needs more study or help. Of course, the punctuation change changes the meaning.

The role of the Jew as good counselor to the wielders of power, and indeed to God, is enshrined in the Bible. Abraham, Moses, Aaron, even Balaam's Ass were all good No. 2s.

God Forbid

When God was angry with the men of S'dom and 'Omorah, and decided to destroy them, it was Abraham who came forward and said, Wilt Thou also destroy the righteous with the wicked. God forbid that you shall do so, to slay the righteous with the wicked and that the righteous shall be as the wicked. God forbid that the Judge of all the earth shall not do justice. (Genesis 18:23-32). My translation—not standard English translation; cholile ('God forbid') can be translated in more dignified fashion as 'far be it from thee' but I prefer this more colloquial version for its unexpectedness.

The Egyptians shall hear it
(A shande (scandal) far di goyim (nations))

When God was angry with the complaints of the Jews in the Wilderness, He said, How long will this people provoke me? I will smite them with the pestilence, and disinherit them. And Moses said unto the Lord: Then the Egyptians shall hear it . . . And they will tell it to the inhabitants of this land . . . Now, if thou shalt kill all this people as one man, then the nations which have heard the fame of thee will speak, saying, Because the Lord was not able to bring this people into the land which he sware unto them, therefore he has slain them in the wilderness. (Numbers 14:11-16).

Shall one man sin?

And the Lord spoke unto Moses and Aaron, saying, Separate yourselves from among this congregation, that I may consume them in a moment. And they fell down upon their faces, and said, O God, . . . shall one man sin and wilt thou be wroth with all the congregation? (Korach, Numbers 16:20-22; cf. Numbers 17:10, "in a moment" 16:45 in the King James version).

Unless she had turned from me

Balaam rode to meet Balak. And God's anger was kindled because he went (having just told him to go), and the angel of the Lord stood in the way for an adversary against him. Now he was riding upon his ass . . . And the ass saw the angel of the Lord standing in the way . . . And the ass turned aside and went into the field; and Balaam smote the ass to turn her into the way . . . And the Lord opened the mouth of the ass, and she said unto Balaam, what have I done unto thee, that thou has smitten me these three times? . . . And the Angel of the Lord said unto him: Wherefore hast thou smitten thine ass these three times? . . . unless she had turned from me, surely now also I had slain thee, and saved her alive. (Numbers 22:20-33).

The point of these stories is not that God is a petulant and irrational wielder of power, although that is indeed what we see here, but that we Jews admire models of speaking truth to power, even divine power.

Think of all the heroes of Jewish tradition who are described as No. 2s:

> Joseph was not a king, but rode in the king's second chariot: (Genesis 41:43)

> Daniel was not a king but the first of three Presidents under Darius. (Daniel vi:3-4, cf. 5:29).

> Mordecai was not a king but second to the King, Ahasueros: (Esther X:3).

> And one translation adds wryly: and accepted by the greater part of his brethren.

In Moorish Spain, Jews were not kings but viziers.[8]

In Russia, Poland, Germany, Jews were superintendents but not lords.

In America, speed writers and advisors with benches in Lafayette Park, across from the White House.

Hasdai ibn Shaprut (915-970) was an advisor to Abd-ar-Rahman III (912-961) and Rahman's son Hakam II (961-   ).

Hasdai was court physician, not vizier, but in effect Minister of Foreign Affairs and Inspector of the Customs for the port of Cordova. He corresponded with the princes of the Khazars, and when their kingdom was overrun, they knew that they would find a welcome from influential people in Spain and went there.[9]

Samuel ibn Nagdala (993-1055), poet, scholar, statesman. After 1020 he was vizier to Habbus of Grenada. He was almost omnipotent. His son Joseph succeeded him. In 1066, however, Jews were attacked.

In Turkey, Joseph Nasi (= prince) (d. 1579) was Duke of Naxos[10]. Roth says "He was able to sway the election of a new king in Poland." There was an interregum in Poland (1572-1573) and Turkey was then a nearer neighbor to Poland than it now seems. Joseph Nasi was succeeded by Solomon Ashkenazi. The election of Henry of Valois to the Polish crown in 1573 had partly been due to his exertions.[11]

In Poland, a Jew, Wahl, was king for a day.

There is a tradition in our family that Leibele Kishiniski, my grandmother's great, great grandfather, was Prime Minister of Poland for a day.[12]

The first story (Wahl) is, I believe, generally accepted but I have not documented it. The second story (Leibele) I have not seen anywhere in print but I have not looked in appropriate places (such as detailed political histories of Poland, if they exist and if I could read them).

If either or both of these stories are true, although they are at first glance surprising, several explanations are possible. My own speculation is this: Polish tradition requires congresses to act by unanimous[13] vote. When a day of debate ended without agreement, both sides agreed upon someone for the temporary position that neither side need fear would attempt to hold on to power in his own right—a Jew. Imagine that we had such a tradition in America. If the Electoral College ended a day without consensus on either Clinton or Dole and felt obligated to have a temporary selection, it would not be Perot, nor Jesse Jackson, but might conceivably be an Arab, Ralph Nader[14]?

Jews were familiar throughout Poland as stewards and administrators of great estates.[15]

In Germany, there were the hofjüden, Joseph Süss Oppenheimer ('Jew Süss'), Gomperz, Fuerst, Goldschmidt.

Jews with important advisory roles include de Luria, de Casseres in Denmark; de Sampaios in Sweden; Lehman, Abensur in Poland; da Costa in Portugal; Boccarro in Spain.

Moses Mendelsohn was on familiar terms with Frederick II, was twitted by him and twitted back. Coming late to dinner at the palace one night, Mendelsohn found at his place a signed note from the Emperor. He looked at it and quietly put it back. Told by the Emperor to read it out loud, he complied and read, Mendelsohn ist *ein* esel. Friedrich der Zweiter. (Mendelsohn is *an* ass. Frederick the *Second*.)

9/18/96

Advisor

Wendell Primus, Peter Edelman, Mary Jo Bane of HHS quit last week, because of Clinton's signing the Republican Welfare bill[16]. They waited until after the Convention. Had I been in their place, I believe I would not have resigned. I would have stayed and done the best I could to ameliorate some of the bad features of the bill. I record this not to say that they were wrong. I think a fairer judgment is that they were right and I would have been wrong, but the incident highlights a difference that I recognize.

9/19/98

Had I been Attorney General at the time of the 'Saturday Night Massacre', when Nixon ordered the firing of Archibald Cox, I believe I would have refused. But had I been Advisor to the Attorney General then, I believe I would have spelled out for the AG the legal grounds that permitted and perhaps justified the firing. Ruckleshaus and Elliot Richardson are my better part, Bork my worser.

3/23/98

Counselor or Scrivener
An example of different roles

A Norwegian lawyer sent me a client who wanted to do business in this country (I purposely do not identify the business). He had selected a representative, let us call him Masaccio (I really don't recall the name). I said, I'll draw a Bishop's Report (a good business report) on him. The client became very angry. "*I* have chosen him. That's a business decision. *You* write the contract." I phoned my Norwegian correspondent and said, Please explain to this client that that is not the way to deal with an American lawyer. He said, that is how Norwegian business men are used to dealing with lawyers. We Norwegians are very stubborn people. He will pay you a good fee. Do as he asks. I said, OK, and I put into the contract a clause (say clause 14) that said in effect that if for any reason it appears that the representative is not able to carry out effectively the representation, we were entitled to rescind the contract. The client was again angry. He said, "That looks as though I do not trust the representative I have chosen." I said, *You* chose the representative. *I* write the contract. The client conceded this was an issue of drafting the contract. The representative and his lawyer had no difficulty with it. The contract was signed. The client paid me a good fee, and went back to Norway.

The next morning, the first page of the New York Times reported that the head of Cosa Nostra in this country having been murdered, the other heads had met at a place called Appalachin to choose a successor. The police, concerned about the sudden convergence of black limousines on this quiet little upstate New York town, raided the house where they were meeting. [My friend Nanette Dembitz thought that an outrageous violation of civil liberties]. A Mr. Masaccio, import representative, was seen jumping out of a window and rushing off. I sent the clipping without comment to my client. A few days later he woke me with a phone call about 6am. Can you get me out of the contract? I said I'll try.

I called Masaccio's lawyer, who agreed that under clause 14 we were entitled to rescind. Send me a rescission and we'll sign it. They had problems enough of course, without adding to it by a fight with us. My Norwegian client paid me a second good fee for getting him out of the contract.

Soon, he reappeared in New York. He had chosen a new representative. I said, let us draw a Bishop's Report. He said, '*I have chosen the representative. That is a business decision. You write the contract.*' I did. He paid me a third good fee. So far as I know, the new representative worked out reasonably well. My Norwegian correspondent was quite right. 'We Norwegians are very stubborn people.'

6/13/96

Experts

A talent that I believe I have and that I believe is somewhat unusual, and that may be Jewish in origin and perhaps connected with the need to correct: the talent of finding errors or weaknesses or fallacies of thought in pronouncements of experts without being one.

For example, accountants are accustomed to intimidating non-experts. Although I am not an accountant nor even a good bookkeeper, one of my talents as a lawyer was that I could ask accountants the right questions to bring out an acknowledgment that a firmly stated conclusion was indeed untenable.

I can also recognize certain weaknesses of medical thinking.

10/7/01

I do not have or claim medical knowledge but I believe I know more than most people about doctors. My father was a house-visiting physician with a remarkable gift for diagnosis. There is, I believe an old medical metaphor that says, when you hear hoof beats, is it horses or zebras. When the attending or specialist physicians said horses and Pop said no, it's zebras, as he often did, it always proved to be zebras (or if he said, not zebras, horses, then horses). Many of our family friends were also physicians. My mother was President of the Physicians' Wives League and my father of the (Masonic) Physicians Square Club. My childhood reading included the magazine Medical Economics and a book called A Book About the Physician Himself[17], also Lives of Pasteur and of Osler. My father organized hospitals and I was a member of the Boards of Directors. When my brother came back from Europe, having run hospitals in addition to other duties as a Red Cross Field Director, he took an examination and became a certified Hospital Administrator and gradually took over my father's responsibilities in our Hospitals.   One of our doctor friends bought a machine from a con artist. The seller demonstrated that it cloned $1 and $10 bills. When it didn't work for him, he complained to the police, not realizing that his complaint was that he was unable to counterfeit.

When I was a child, tonsillectomy was a favorite procedure. My father did not approve because he believed the tonsils served a purpose and it was better to save them if possible. I think that is now an accepted view.

Military surgeons once believed that blood was good, and practiced transfusions. Then they learned that blood came in types and the wrong type could be bad, so they transfused only appropriate types. But they also learned that there was an rh factor, and so on. Of course, that is how science grows but the growth of science is a secondary goal, not a primary goal of medicine. The premature enthusiasm of physicians for incomplete knowledge meanwhile did harm. When Irma studied nutrition she learned that shrimp was bad because it contained cholesterol. The next generation learned that there was good cholesterol and bad cholesterol and shrimp was good because it contributed to good cholesterol, was low in saturated fat, and contained Omega 3 fatty acid. And so on. In government, at OEO, I was the lawyer for the OEO's Medical Program. In HEW as Special Counsel to the General Counsel, I dealt with inconsistencies of Medicare and Medicaid regulation; and I was lawyer for the Long Term Care Office. And later as Chairman of the Departmental Grant Appeals Board, I dealt with many medical cases as well as others.

I believe that my familiarity with doctors' ways of thinking often enables me to spot medical error without having medical knowledge. Compare Feynman's tragic story of the death of his wife Arlene from lymphatic tuberculosis, a disease readily diagnosed but that was falsely diagnosed as Hodgkin's disease. The one physician who asked the right questions was treated as a trouble-maker. *What Do YOU Care What Other People Think* (Large Print, G.V. Hall, Boston) 40-71.

6/13/96

Shipping Archives

Another example, in a Chapter X bankruptcy case in Florida: The holder of shipping archives in New york had been instructed by the Trustee, on orders of the Court, to show me any records I asked for. I believed the Trustee had been engaged in misconduct by coziness with those who had caused the loss of the company's principal ship, and I hoped that the ship's archives would help prove their responsibility for the loss. The Trustee knew that that was what I was after. I believe the Trustee instructed the holder of the archives by telephone, indicating with a wink that the less they showed me, the better he would be pleased. Of course, I cannot prove it. How do you prove a wink over a telephone.

The archive staff showed me some innocuous files. I asked for more. They said that was the entire file on the ship involved. I asked about the structure of the system of files and pointed out that the existence of these files implied the existence of others. They then admitted there were more and brought them out. Again, I asked for more. Again, they said that's all. We went through this four times. They finally produced a file with the evidence I had hoped to find, but only when I showed that the file structure proved it had to exist.

A further clinching proof of the Trustee's involvement was produced by my wife Irma. This story is it not told in my book on coincidences. It earned her the sotto voce title "Witch". [18] [The trustee was discharged with a sour comment by the Judge that he didn't need us to show him the Trustee's misconduct].

This talent was also shown by my teacher and friend Mortimer Adler. He had it, generally, in a higher degree than I did. In his case and in mine, it rested on a strong sense of logical structure. Experts in a subject matter may know much more than we did about the substance, but not perceive as clearly as we did the necessary logical relations of pieces of knowledge they had or pretended to have. Mortimer applied this talent to psychology, in which he did have expertise; to law, in which he did not (notably law of evidence and criminal law); to editing the Encyclopaedia Britannica, in which, as perhaps was to be expected, he did a distinctive and impressive but flawed job. His talent was a great strength, but it was also a weakness.

Mortimer, in my opinion, severely harmed a generation of Columbia Law students (in the 1930's) by persuading a well-informed lawyer with great practical experience (Professor J.M.) to jettison his knowledge and communicable skills in favor of a not altogether sound symbolic logic analysis of evidence law which the instructor never fully grasped and no one in the class other than I had the training to evaluate. (Without directly confronting Mortimer's approach, I have indicated what I believe are some of its deficiencies[19] in my articles A Theory of Contract Sanctions, and The Logical Structure of a Proposition of Law).

Mortimer was a student of Thomas Aquinas and, I think, nominally a Catholic[20] (as I was for a very brief period), but of course we were both Jews and I attribute the flaws to Aristotle and the skills to Maimonides and Spinoza rather than Aquinas.

The essence of our talent was the combination of a wide acquaintance with miscellaneous knowledge and a meta—(meta-logical, meta-physical) overview of the structure of science.

I think it is not surprising that many paradigm changers were Jews: Einstein, Freud, Feynman.

4/7/95

There were two men in a chimney

One of my problems—I do not say it is a weakness, but it would impair me as a politician, had I wanted to be a politician—is a tendency to see that there may be merit in an opposing view. Another, perhaps closely related, is a tendency to have opinions that are too complicated.

A simple example. Many people think Anita Hill lied and therefore Clarence Thomas was rightly confirmed as a Justice of the Supreme Court.

Many people think Anita Hill told the truth and therefore Thomas was wrongly confirmed.

I believed Anita Hill told substantially the truth, and Thomas, I am sure, from his conduct (notably his deliberate absence from the hearing, when as an experienced lawyer he must have known that confronting her with a yellow pad and pencil in his hand would be an effective deterrent if she were lying and a useful basis for cross examination and rebuttal) lied about her. But I don't believe his sexual pressures on her make a compelling reason not to confirm him. The lying about it does, somewhat, but is understandable and perhaps forgivable. Yet I do not think he should have been confirmed. The reason, however, is not his lying about Anita Hill, nor even his lying about Roe v. Wade, of which I think he was also obviously guilty. He should not have been confirmed because he is not a competent judge. (My friend MF, however, a competent observer, has reviewed Thomas' decisions on the Court of Appeals and disagrees with me).

Where most people have a two line position, I have a sixteen line position. That is quite typical.

It is also somewhat typical of Jewish intellectuals generally.

Hear Now

A Christian scholar once wanted to study Talmud. The Talmudist, a friend, when pressed, said reluctantly, I'm afraid you don't have a head for it.

Christian scholar: !

Talmudist: Hear now. There were two men in a chimney. They fell down into the soot at the bottom of the chimney.

	When they got up, one was clean, one was dirty. Which one went to wash?
C.S.:	The dirty one, of course.
T.:	The dirty man would look at the clean man and think, How lucky, we are still clean. The clean man would look at the dirty one and think, Wow, are we dirty. So which one went to wash?
C.S.:	Very clever. I see. The clean one went to wash.
T.:	Of course, the clean one would start to go, but the dirty one would say to him, why are you going? You are clean. The clean one would say, Oh, but you are dirty.
C.S.:	Oh, that double twist is very nice. I like that.
T.:	So, there were two men in a chimney. They both fell down into the soot at the bottom of the chimney. Which one went to wash?
C.S.:	Well, now if I say the dirty one, you say the clean one. If I say the clean one, you say the dirty one. What shall I answer?
T.:	You see, you don't have a head for it. There were two men in a chimney and they both fell down into the soot at the bottom. How can one be clean and one be dirty?

7/24-25/96

In the first chapter of this book, ('Meno'), and later, I made a strong distinction between Platonists and Aristotelians.[21] As the

French sometimes say, Je me comprends. I know what I mean. For the purpose of that discussion, the distinction is good enough. I relied on a fairly crude and public conception, and carefully abstained from qualifying it. Had I expressed myself there more accurately, how needlessly complex those earlier sections would have become. So I have reserved doing so until here, when this book is under way.

I used Aristotle as a symbol for the literal, static thinking that later characterized Aristotelian scholasticism, after the Greek was translated into Arabic and into Latin. That is not the Aristotle whose emphasis was always on the dynamic, on the becoming.

Aristotle was not an Aristotelian. Andronikos, the editor of what has come down to us as the Aristotelian corpus, was, I suppose, an Aristotelian. Aristotle was not an Aristotelian. He was a Platonist, and particularly on the point I was writing about: that learning is a kind of reminding[22]. Plato, I suspect, but it is hard to be sure, was no Platonist. He was a Socratic.

If I were to defend this thesis, although it should be obvious to careful readers, I would have to write a book. I can put that book on the list of a dozen or two dozen books I have meant to write[23].

See how a fairly simple and, I think, valid point would have been lost in complexity if I had tried to say some of this in those first pages. Yet my impulse to correct, to qualify, to avoid implications I don't intend, is very strong. I have to fight against it. I do not do well on true-false tests because I am too fertile in thinking of exceptions and qualifications. I have to learn to be simple-minded.

5/4/98

Managing

Executive style calls for an in-basket and an out-basket. For each issue that needs decision, decide it. Very little should go to a pending-basket, and then only for reasons beyond my control.

That is not the style I am most comfortable with. My pending-basket gets most issues. My whole house has become my pending-basket—every horizontal surface, bed, table, dresser, sofa, chair, floor. There is, I believe, a conflict between the artistic and the executive. I can do both. I have done an executive job when I had to. But the style I am most comfortable with is to let things sit, marinate, find unexpected connections later on.

My executive skills peaked about 1949 when I was General Counsel of the Office of Alien Property[24] and about 1975 when I was Chairman of the HEW Departmental Grant Appeals Board. I did decide and I did create. But I much prefer holding things, in order to keep looking at them in new lights.

Such executive training as I have had comes first from my mother who taught me, Let your head save your heels.[25]

From my sister, who taught me, but not successfully, organization and dispositiveness.

From my teacher John Schamus, who taught me to organize materials that I might need for later use.[26]

From my uncle Herman who taught me business routines and the value of prompt action, (in those ancient days we used to take a 5% discount for paying bills promptly, as practice then permitted). Our camp on Raquette Lake was known throughout the Adirondacks and beyond for its excellent credit. Any Greylock counselor could go anywhere and say charge it to Camp Greylock.

From my uncle Gabe for whom, one summer, floating in a flat-bottomed boat in Center Lake, I served as amanuensis while he organized teachers' assignments. (This one has seniority, but this one is a better teacher, but this one should be available to coach the debating team . . . .)

And then from an excellent short training course at the Federal Executive Institute in Charlottesville. Excellent except for its failure to describe correctly the federal grant system. I tried later to persuade the Institute and the Office of Personnel Management to correct this but without success.

It is popular to gibe at government employees, Have you ever met a payroll? Well, yes, I have, running camp, sharing in running hospitals, a laundry, a Uranium mine, serving on the boards of major corporations. Despite the popular opinion, the Office of Alien Property proved that government *could* run corporations with conspicuous success.[27]

6/16/95

Aza stobbrich a man

That is an expression Jack Karro told me his father (a Kurlander) used to use. So stubborn a man. So far as I know, it is not a standard Yiddish expression. I think Jack's father had a general habit of interlarding his Yiddish with non-Yiddish words. (vis-a-vis . . . meaning 'across de strit').

My mother said we Masons were a stubborn bunch. No doubt she said the Kahns were also. I suppose she meant primarily her father,—and herself.

When I was—what? 6?—I refused chocolate pudding one night. I loved chocolate pudding (My-T-Fine). Why did I refuse it that night, I don't know. My mother unwisely said she would put it in the icebox and keep it until I did eat it. I never ate it. After weeks, she had to throw it out because it was bad. On my mother's part, this was foolish and uncharacteristic. Was it Kahn stubbornness? No doubt some deeper clash lay behind this since both of us acted contrary to our norms. Was it because of Irv's birth when I was 5.

At Evander Childs High School (about 1923?), I was outstanding in chemistry, but I did not keep a notebook because 'it did not suit my method of learning.' (I have never kept course notebooks, in high school, in college, in law school, in training courses). But I got 100 on every weekly test. To 'teach me a lesson', the chemistry teacher flunked me at midterm. Midterm grades are ordinarily no more than indicators of where improvement may be needed. The same thing happened in biology for the same reason. By probably a coincidence, I was also flunked at midterm (inappropriately) by a French teacher whose pronunciation I had corrected. Under a school rule, flunking three subjects, I had to drop something. I dropped chemistry and biology. My chemistry teacher and my biology teacher begged me not to do that, but I insisted and did. As a result, I did not become a physician, although perhaps my distaste for dissection might have blocked me anyway. The lack of high school biology and chemistry forced me to take an elementary science course in college. I took geology, and again got weekly "A"s. (Perhaps I could have been excused from the elementary science by taking advanced placement examinations. I did in English and I think in French, but they didn't have that in science, or I didn't know it, or was still being stubborn). After completing a year of elementary geology, I registered for a doctorate level course in geology with the approval of the Professor, Douglas Johnson, a distinguished physiographer. But the Bursar refused to let the course be given for a single undergraduate. So I never became a geologist either. I had no interest in the intermediate courses.

The high school librarian said I had failed to return a book I had borrowed. I said her records were wrong. She wanted me suspended from school—I was suspended (I remember speculating that that might mean the end of my academic career). The High School principal, Henry Norr, friend of my uncle Gabe and father of my chum Milton (Martin) Norr, urged me to apologize. "Sometimes we have to learn to swallow injustices". I refused to apologize because I had not said anything that was not true. I don't know how the matter was resolved. Obviously, the suspension was terminated, because I graduated. I am not sure, but I have a feeling that when Henry Norr said, sometimes we have to learn, there was an undercurrent of 'sometimes we Jews have to learn . . . '

The Explosion of the Carib Queen

In the 1950s, I undertook a litigation which lasted some twenty years of stubborn, imaginative, and until the end of the road, unpaid effort. This was a corporate reorganization precipitated by the explosion at sea of the company's principal vessel, the result, I believed, of improvident management decisions made in the interest of stock manipulations. I was joined by my friend Irwin Langbein as local counsel in Florida and by my wife Irma, who started as my assistant but contributed crucially to the case. When we appealed the District Court's plan of reorganization, we wanted Irma's name on the brief. That required that she be admitted to the appellate court's bar. That was then the Fifth Circuit (later split into two Circuits). One of our opponents was TriContinental, but it probably did not oppose us in this appeal. It was represented by Claude Pepper who had been U.S. Senator from Florida. He offered to move her admission and did so in a very flowery style, referring to Irma as "our little Portia". Pepper later became a member of the House. About 25 years later I had lunch with Chip Pashayan, Representative from California. We ate in the Members Dining Room. Chip had been a special Assistant to the General Counsel of HEW, rooming next door to me and sharing a secretary. As we ate, Claude Pepper came by. I got up and introduced myself. Pepper said, Of course, I remember you, *and how is your wife*? Is that a politician's extraordinary memory of people or a politician's skillful bluff?

We were told by many experts (peripatetics) that our case was hopeless: There was nothing for stockholders (whom we represented). The United States District Court treated us badly and insisted contemptuously that there was no value for the stockholders. The United States Court of Appeals sent the case back twice, but the third time the unanimous Court of Appeals ruled against us, and it was a good court, too. We asked the United States Supreme Court to review the case. This review was discretionary. The issues in the case were traditionally within the District Court's authority to decide; the District Judge and a unanimous Court of Appeals had ruled against us; no one was sitting in jail; there was no constitutional issue.

The Solicitor General's Office, although conceding that we were right in principle, refused to support our request for review because it was obvious that our case was hopeless and it would impair the prestige of the Solicitor General to be seen supporting such a hopeless case.

Yet we persuaded the Supreme Court to review the case, and then to reverse the Court of Appeals (390 U.S. 414). We asked for and got a new Judge, a new Trustee, a new Trustee's counsel. A somewhat Pyrrhic victory: we had to take 14 more appeals (I haven't counted recently but I think 14), and won all but one that was held to be moot (that is, no longer in controversy). Ultimately we obtained three and a half million dollars for the stockholders and a disgracefully small fee for ourselves, having angered the new District Judge by getting him repeatedly reversed.

By a wild coincidence, Irma happened to learn of and get a copy of the Supreme Court decision in our favor before the Solicitor General's Office did, and had the pleasure of phoning them to tell them that we had won the case they had said was hopeless. [This too is spelled out in my chapter on Coincidences, which is not part of this volume].

Stiff-necked

The Bible repeatedly says we Jews are a stiff-necked, stiff-hearted people. Exodus 32.9. And the Lord said unto Moses, I have seen this people, and, behold, it is a stiff-necked people. [golden calf]

> Ex 33.3, 5: for thou art a stiff-necked people
>
> Ex 34.9: Moses to God: For it is a stiff-necked people, and pardon our inequity and our sin, and take us for thine inheritance.
>
> Deut. 9.13: Behold, it is a stiff-necked people. Let me alone, that I may destroy them . . .
>
> Deut 10.16 circumcise . . . your heart and be no more stiff-necked
>
> Ezek 2.4 For they are impudent children and stiff-hearted
>
> Psalms 75.5: Speak not with a stiff neck.

The Bible says this disparagingly and with a reverse meaning: weak in our adherence to Jewish principle, but had we not been stiff-necked and strong in our Jewishness, would we have survived at all or survived as a people, these thousands of years? Or have we survived rather, as Henry Norr may have thought, by learning to swallow injustices? Both have some truth.

Although, as I have said earlier, my family deliberately eschewed the use of Yiddish so that the children would grow up speaking only an un-yiddish-inflected English, nevertheless, once I think of these things, words and phrases come back to me that I know I heard as a child[28]. A stubborn person was called an aksh or an akshn. I thought it was a distortion of the English word ox. (No doubt I vaguely recognized that it was somehow Jewish. In fact, akshan, is a regular Hebrew word for a stubborn person and it is used in Yiddish with the pronunciation akshn).

When I was a teenager at camp, my bed and trunk were sloppier than most. My uncle George (I suspect he was assigned by a family council) told me that was unacceptable. Especially because the Masons were directors of the camp, for a Mason to so violate the standards was embarrassing. I agreed and promised to make my bed and trunk neat, but then I would not sleep there. I would sleep in the woods and let the neat bunk stay neat. My uncle agreed, probably thinking I would not carry it out very long. He imposed a condition that at least once a day I report for line-up (presence check before meals). I spent the summer sleeping in the woods. He should have known how stubborn a Mason can be.

3/13/95

My daughter, Jan, said I was stubborn, which is correct. She added that she was. My mother and I long agreed that the stubbornness is inherited.

Naive Intellectualism

Through all my work, there is a strain of naïve intellectualism. Often I act on the basis of accepting as real other people's rationalizations or intellectual arguments.

Example: My boyhood friend, Walter Surrey, for the Board of Economic Warfare and for the Department of State, urged certain post-World War II arrangements on the ground that if European and American interests were economically involved with each other, that would be a powerful encouragement of world peace. The idea, I thought, was sound. When I then proposed the creation of an international corporation in which the capital would be supplied by the various allied nations out of German assets seized in the war, I expected Department of State support. They did not fight me but they did not support me either. They permitted me to present the idea at an international meeting with credentials as an American representative. But without active support, the idea foundered.

When I proposed a plan to obtain Iranian oil in the time of Mossadegh (1950-51) without appearing to give political support to Mossadegh, the Department of State rejected the proposal. Here, I should have understood that the Department (unwisely in my view) wanted Mossadegh's downfall rather than merely avoidance of political encouragement. The result, I think, was the Shah's continuance and thus Khomeini.

Another example. In 1947, the idea of "Europe" was beginning to bubble in advanced circles, particularly French: Schumann, Monnet, Rueff, Marion; Benelux; the Council of Europe (1949), the Coal and Iron Cooperation (1953). There was also an Economic study organization in Geneva; with the European Community (1958) and the Parliament on the horizon, and the International Atomic Energy Agency. I was sensitive to this intellectual current, but less sensitive to the unspoken but equally real tensions moving the other way—French nationalism, anti-Britishism, anti-Americanism. These were less intellectual, more emotional, more cultural, and I was less aware of them.

An Assistant Secretary for Personnel called a meeting of managers and said, I want you to be tough. If an employee misbehaves or makes an unjustified claim, you have to say so, and I will back you up.   An employee misbehaved rather blatantly. Her Supervisor (not I) said so. The employees union filed a grievance. I was surprised. I thought the union would see the employee was clearly in the wrong and that the union's effectiveness would be increased by not supporting outrageous claims. I was wrong. The union was more interested in being on the side of the employee, no matter what the merits. The case was appealed. The Assistant Secretary supported the union. " . . . and I will back you up"—hah!   So I was wrong again. The Assistant Secretary saw more benefit to himself in friendly relations with the Union than in the respect of the managers he had urged to be tough. I had been naïve indeed to believe his strong urging to be tough. Gov't Admin., 101: never believe an Assistant Secretary for Personnel. After all, how did he get there?

De Weg Naar Maastricht, alsdublieft

In 1947, a Canadian colonel and his wife and driver took me by bombed-out roads from Brussels to Berlin. I had been ordered to return to Washington at once, but my brother, whom I had only briefly seen for the duration of the War was in Berlin as Advisor to General Clay on Internal Restitution and I was not going to go home without seeing him. The Canadian Colonel wrote me travel orders directing me to go to Berlin and then took me there. Until we got into Germany and the Autobahn, my duty was to jump out at every doubtful fork in the road and ask, De weg naar Maastricht, alsdublieft? The way to Maastricht, if you please? This usually got a cheerful laugh as well as a gestured direction. A conference at Maastricht (1991) established the European Union with 15 or so members and about 345 million people.

2/26/95

Myths

We Jews have a talent for making compelling myths—Paul, the Christian myth, Marx, the Communist myth, Freud, the psychotherapeutic myth,—that have conquered the world.

We also have a talent for dividing and subdividing our myths. This talent is not exclusively Jewish but I think we excel in it.

Freud's friends, Jewish and Swiss, English, American, quickly established orthodoxies and heresies in great number: Freud, Adler, Jung, Horney, Klein . . . Marx's followers: Trotskyites, Lovestoneites, Left Deviationists, Right Deviationists . . . Christian non-Jewish schisms were many: Greek, Russian, Coptic, Armenian, Cathars, Huss, Wycliff, Henry VIII, Amish, Mennonites, Knox, Wesley, Southern Baptists, Northern Baptists, National Baptists, many over the centuries, but just in the life-time of Paul, see how many different Jewish Christian views there were of non-Jewish Christians.[29]

Perhaps every compelling myth carries with it a tendency to form schisms. But the presence of Jews in many of them, I think may reinforce that tendency.

American democracy perhaps has had fewer major schisms than most in 200 years—slave belt, free belt; sun belt, snow belt, rust belt; farmer, labor, industry and an increasing Republican-Democratic immorality.

Among Jewish divisions: those who were carried away, those who never left, those who came back, those who didn't come back; Pharisees, Saducees; Essenes; Karaites; Sephardim, Ashkenazim; Chsidim, Misnagdim; Haskala, assimilationists, anti-assimilationists; orthodox, reform, conservative, reconstructionist, feminist, Zionist, anti-Zionist, and more.

2/18/95

Where there are two Jews, there are three opinions. A Jewish Robinson Crusoe rescued after many years, before leaving his island took his rescuers on a tour, showing them his sleeping quarters, his storage place, and his two synagogues. That? Why that is the synagogue I don't go to. (Every Jew must have a synagogue he doesn't go to.)

Es iz shver tzu zain a yid
(It is tough to be a Jew)

At Wilkowishk, about 85 km southeast of Tilsit, and about 70km southwest of Kovno, Napoleon called together my grandmother's great great grandfather (Leibele Kishinishki) and other town notables. He apologized for an abuse of the synagogue by his quartermaster, who had, without his knowledge, he said, stabled the Emperor's horses there. (Shtetl synagogues often had dirt floors, and perhaps were thus convenient for stabling). Napoleon added, You Jews will never be fairly treated until you fight your way to Jerusalem.[30]

Jews have been murdered, raped, robbed, burnt, excluded, carried away, forcibly baptized, trickily baptized (as when a house maid, on being discharged, alleged that she had secretly baptized the child of the family, who therefore, as a Christian, could no longer live with its parents and would be punished as a heretic if it lapsed to Jewish ways).[31]

Most of us in America are descendants of those who fled specific waves of pogroms. My grandparents came in 1890 and 1891, a time of major troubles. But here in America there has been relatively little violence against Jews—much latent anti-Semitism, some overt anti-Semitism (Ku Klux Klan, Father Coughlin, much anti-government, anti-capitalist, anti-Communist talk and some action enriched by anti-Semitism), but little outright violence.

When I grew up here, it was largely peripheral. There were hotels that would not take Jews, hotels that might not take Jews (better be sure), housing developments where the buyer covenanted not to sell to Jews, clubs that did not admit Jews, fraternities that excluded Jews. Good colleges and professional schools had numerical limits on the number of Jews they would admit (except City College, New York). Many doctors had had to get their medical training in Scotland because Columbia-Presbyterian would not take them beyond a quota. Major Bar Associations would not take Jews. The Bar Association of the City of New York did not, I believe. The New York County Lawyers Association, which did, was created by a non-Jew who deplored the exclusion. The New York Athletic Club, I understand, preferred to exclude Jews. My uncle Chuck was a member, perhaps as a token, or perhaps as a crack in the door.

Jews, Italians, Irish found it hard to get capital loans. The Bank of Italy (Bank of America) and Amalgamated Bank were created to meet some of this problem.

Of course Blacks and Hispanics, have encountered these discriminations and very much worse, with somewhat different dynamics.

Over the years, most of the open anti-Jewish discrimination has evaporated, although anti-Semitism remains as a potent energy.

I have been aware of these things but have been little affected by them. When I was recommended for the position of General Counsel of the Office of Alien Property Custodian, I didn't get it until after a non-Jew, because 'it wouldn't look right' for me to follow Raoul Berger—'two Jews in a row'. No one, of course, worried about two Catholics in a row, or two Badgers in a row. But it's a minor gall.

11/29/96

Anti-Semitism in Law Practice

There is a special kind of anti-Semitism that I have encountered in law practice, especially in the South. Jews are disliked and mistreated *except* when they are seen to be scoundrels, dishonest, overreaching, money-motivated. Those who meet this exceptional test of confirming anti-Jewish prejudices may be welcomed and favored.

If this observation is correct, and I believe it is, the explanation is not difficult. A dominant group ('good ol' boys') can use such Jews to serve their own less avowable ends, while still feeling superior. If we can only feel that you Jews are, as a Jew should be, dirtier than we are, we'll give you your tens of thousands and take our larger share more comfortably. Judges will favor you if you will do the dirty work for their drinking buddies, and the Bar will understand and approve. I believe the injustices perpetrated in the District Court in the TMT case were motivated in part that way.

There is a widely used national listing and rating of lawyers. My distaste for this listing stems primarily from the loss by my friend Irwin Langbein of his top rating. He had it when he was a member of a firm in which the first named partner was a deservedly respected non-Jew. When the first named partner died, the firm lost its top rating, although all the legitimate reasons for the rating (ability, financial solidity, high standards) were still there. The problem, I am convinced, was that my friend was outstandingly competent and successful and unimpeachably honorable. For a Jew to be abler than thou, and sensitively honorable, was not tolerable to the leading members of the local Bar whose consensus supported the ratings.

Apologia Pro "Vita" Sua

No doubt there is an infusion of vanity here in my writing this book, along with, I believe, mostly a base of self-awareness.

This is an undistinguished life told in a perspective of Jewish tradition, that I may not have right. I am not a learned nor a piously observant Jew. If I were, I might have something to contribute on Jewish thinking or Jewish history because of my learning or my piety. I am not a great American, no world shaker nor a participant observer of the shaking, to contribute insights into American and world history.

My place in the world is perhaps neatly imaged by grades of formal power. I was in next to the lowest rank of lawyers in the Agricultural Adjustment Administration, subordinate to Telford Taylor, Frank Shea, Alger Hiss, Jerome Frank, and Henry Wallace, and a co-worker of Abe Fortas, all appropriately famous. Litigation Supervisor in the National Labor Relations Board, a lesser position than it sounds, subordinate to an Assistant General Counsel (Larry Knapp), Associate General Counsel (Garry Van Arkel, Alvin Rockwell), Deputy General Counsel (Bob Watts), and to General Counsel (Charles Fahy) and to the Board. General Counsel of the Office of Alien Property, reporting to the Assistant Attorney General (David Bazelon) and to the Attorney General (Tom C. Clark); and Special Assistant to the Attorney General. I was Associate General Counsel of the Office of Economic Opportunity, subordinate to the Deputy General Counsel, to the General Counsel, and to the Director (Sargent Shriver and successors). Special Counsel for Regulatory Matters to the General Counsel, Department of Health, Education, and Welfare; then Chairman of HEW Departmental Grant Appeals Board, reporting to the Under-Secretary and Secretary. A practicing lawyer in New York, not very successful professionally or financially.

8/8/97

I offered an economic program to the President of the United States supported by the Attorney General, but my scheduled meeting with the President (Truman) was canceled and my program never adopted.

In 1931, I sat in a café in Rome with a fascist official and heard him bad mouth Mussolini publicly and loudly. (Would he or I end up drinking castor oil? Or was he instructed to start up such talk to see who would agree?)

I have never even met a State Governor—except Ribicoff when he was in Congress and I went to persuade him to do something any decent person should have agreed to, in my view (extend the time limit for persons persecuted by the Nazis to reclaim property that had been seized on the assumption that they were Germans). He refused to introduce a bill to that effect. "What's in it for my constituents?"

I have never met even a Mayor, except the Mayor of Selma, Alabama. He was polite and even cordial, seemingly trying to persuade me that his actions toward Blacks were proper. After I got back, I was in Don Baker's office when a Senator from Alabama called Baker and said, What the hell do you mean sending a nigger to Selma to investigate? Baker replied, Senator, I think you have it wrong. The only one who should complain is an Arab. [I don't say which Senator. I think I know, but 25 years later or so, Don Baker says I am wrong and that the Senator I think it was would never have spoken like that.]

I did, however, work with Ed Koch on local elections in Manhattan before he was Mayor.

7/6/97

I am not Prince Hamlet

I did not participate in the Iran-Conta scandal and coverup nor in the uncovering of it nor did I know directly any of those who did, except tangentially two, Meese and Weinberger. I did know well many who did know well those who did participate in the two sides of this. This pattern is repeated through many important events of my time.

8/8/97

I met Ambassadors, participated in minor diplomatic negotiations, had foreign officials as personal friends, proposed international programs that were adopted but were never important; proposed in the time of Mossadegh a program for dealing with Iran and the oil supply that was rejected; proposed a program for dealing with OPEC-created oil shortages that was rejected because FEA, the Federal Energy Administration, did not think there was an emergency ('we have nothing to fear but FEA itself'). I was invited to a reception by the Queen of Belgium but rejected it because I was offended by a requirement that I wear (that is, rent) white tie (I now think I was not justified, although at the time several very conservative foreign diplomats told me they agreed with me, having in mind the distance I had come). Feynman attended and described a Belgian Royal reception—probably a more prestigious one than the one I was invited to attend. *What Do YOU care What Other People Think* 117-123. I had a meeting scheduled with the dictator of Nicaragua, but he kept postponing it day by day until I gave up and went home.

I add for amusement that in the 1950s my wife and I and our friend Jan Elbogen, returning to Frankfort by dusty Volkswagen from a vacation in Kitzbühl, sat with composure at a good table in a hotel dining room in the Vierjahreszeiten in München in our travel clothes, along with the Pretender to the Throne of Austria, the Patriarch of Jerusalem, a Cardinal or two and other high dignitaries of the Catholic Church in full dress. Irma was, I believe, the only woman in the dining room. We had driven up to the hotel and were told there were no rooms. It was Eucharist Week. All the hotels in München were filled. Jan asked for the manager. The manager came and, seeing Jan, said, Oh, Herr Elbogen, for you, of course we have rooms. So we had two excellent rooms, the manager's reserve. In the aftermath of the War, Jan, serving in the American Army, had been Military Government officer in charge of the hotel industry.   The next morning, the Eucharist Week had ended. The dignitaries left, one by one in great limousines. Worshipful crowds lined the hotel driveway. As our dusty beetle pulled out of the garage, the crowd wondered who we could be and would surely have kissed our rings if we had put our hands out of the car window.

11/29/96

I have been near the outer edge but never at the heart of great events. While many Jews are neither learned nor pious, their history, not only that of the most imbued, make up Jewish history. Most Americans are not world shakers. Their history, not only that of the most powerful and admirable or detestable, make up American history.

The conviction that what an individual does and sees reflects something of his community is true even for those who are not in the extremes of influence (or its lack) but somewhere in the middle.

I write in part out of the conviction that what happens to any of us shows something of the whole world, if we can see it, and I try to see it or show some of it.

6/14/95

My knowledge of Jewish tradition and Jewish history is weak. My own achievements and importance minor. My insights are not startling. Had any of these been great, they would serve as a reason for writing this book. But they are not.

Then why do I write it. Perhaps some others will find it of interest for an unusual crosscutting of the insights of an alert mind that has not done great things but has been able to observe them and to know many of those who have done them and that has not been deeply imbued in Jewish thinking but has been interested in learning more. Then, because I enjoy writing it and because it helps me to organize my own thinking about these matters and to bring my life to a close by the writing of a coda. Then, because my family, my grandchildren especially, may find it of some interest to have their lives placed in a context of their forebears (of their grandfather, that is, and of the part of their family history I can write about).

12/1/96

Although never an important or successful politician, I have had an active role in political campaigns and understand something of political cuisine. I have participated in the drafting of statutes that were enacted and in the interpretation and enforcement of statutes. I have been a bureaucrat at many levels short of Presidential appointment and have seen how bureaucracy works behind the scenes. Not an advocate of distinction, I have tried cases, argued appeals, won some, lost some I should have won, and given good counsel to clients thinking of litigating.

1/22/97

I have been the subject of first page Wall Street Journal news that I believe was willfully distorted, first page New York Times news that was fair and even favorable, and several Wall Street Journal items that were friendly.

8/10/97

Upper Lower

In many ways, I am in the top of the bottom or the bottom of the top.

My IQ, whatever it measures, is no doubt high but not, I assume, extremely so. (I don't know what it is). I was gifted in mathematics and somewhat creative, but did not pursue that path and was never outstanding. I was a solid chess player but not brilliant. Now (after a long period of not playing and, with age, a diminution of my insight), I can usually but not always solve two-move problems and sometimes, but most often not, three-movers. My end game skills were never sufficiently developed.

Financially, I have more money than most but am not in a class with the rich. Some of what I have derives from inheritance, from my father, my bachelor uncles. My income from law practice was inadequate. In government, I was for many years at the top of the Civil Service scale (P-8), then when supergrades were introduced, at the bottom of the supergrades (16?), then in the Senior Executive Service. I have never been in the levels that require Senate confirmation. Psychologically, I came of age in the Depression years and do not spend money easily, but I do not think I am miserly.

My people-skills are weak. I am socially inept. I am polite to others and concerned about their feelings but not naturally gifted in awareness, and not naturally generous or charitable. I am not brave but I do not think I am a coward.

My strength is as the strength of eight, because my heart is pure.[32]

6/1/95

Chapters of the Fathers

Pirkey Oves, or in the now more popular Israeli pronunciation, Pirkey Abot, the Chapters of the Fathers, sometimes called Ethics of the Fathers, is a section of the Talmud that includes some generalized, sometimes delphic, life advice attributed to the early rabbis, and, among other things several anecdotes reflecting the contrast between the patient Hillel and the irascible Shammai, of the period of Jesus' youth.

Among its teachings is the saying of which my wife Irma was very fond—she embossed it on tape and attached it to the shelves above her desk—"If I am not for myself, who will be" (this may have reflected Irma's consciousness of her own too weak self-respect) "if I am only for myself, what am I? And if not now, when?"

Another of its teachings: "Do not separate yourself from the community and its interests."

I am something of a loner by nature. My son is or has become more so. My own path has been, I think, outward from my solitude toward the community and I recognize some of the influences that have led that way.

This saying reflects the Jewish value on the community. That value is real. Jews are preeminent in their creation of community organizations of interaid: Society of immigrants from specific areas of Europe; Society to provide dowries for marriageable girls; Society for visiting the sick; Society for burying the dead; Society for free loans; Society for ransoming prisoners. Unlike Blue Cross or United Way, the officers of such societies did not get salaries or plush perks. They did get respect, sometimes grudgingly. Jews are prominent in organizing study groups and lectures, in establishing scholarships, in supporting museums, theatres, symphonies (Nixon's: 'The Arts, they're Jews'). I do not stress the big contributions made by wealthy Jews (Rothschild, Montefiore, Rosenwald, Silverman in Philadelphia, Kreeger in Washington) as much as the outpouring of small support from the unwealthy. Even the very poor put coins in a 'pushke'(a can with a coin slot) to support a yeshiva (a talmudic school). Jews are by tradition givers to the community, socialists, liberals, communists, democrats.

Or does this saying reflect on the contrary that there is in our make-up a tendency to isolation that needs to be cured? Perhaps that too.

I never go to class reunions—high school, college, law school.

On the other hand, I faithfully try to go to the Office of Alien Property annual lunch, and I gladly meet with Office of Economic Opportunity staff. I faithfully attend the lunches of the Legal and Financial Discussion group every Friday if at all possible.

My uncle Gabe was a conspicuous adherent and creator and officer of groups: Wordsworth Society, City College Alumni Association, Emerson Society, University Settlement, City College Club, the Socialist Party, Teachers Union (1912), Elijah D. Clark Junior High School, Abraham Lincoln High School, High School Principals Association, Jewish Teachers Community Chest, Camp Greylock for Boys, American Philosophical Association, the Spinoza Institute, the League for Industrial Democracy, the Liberal Party, the Ethical Culture Society.

Although my temperament seems in that respect quite opposed to his, my resume shows objectively some small element of that kind of activity. Although subjectively no joiner, I was a Democratic Precinct Captain, Law Chairman of the Riverside Reform Democrats, then Chairman of the Riverside Reform Democrats, delegate to New York State Constitutional Convention, Reform Movement candidate for Democratic County Chairman (Manhattan); organizer of the Stockholders Protective Committee of TMT, Advisor to the Departmental Grant Appeals Board and then its first full time Chairman, creator (at the suggestion of Paul Dembling) of the Federal Bar Association Federal Grants Committee, sponsor (with Paul Dembling) of an American Bar Association Federal Assistance Committee (later abolished by the ABA in its parochial ignorance), active in many ways in creating recognition of the law of grants as a topic of study and practice.

My strong preference in law practice has always been to be active where I feel I am doing something useful to the community.

I have skills in government work. I have never wanted (except as part of my bildungsroman) to work where the rewards are money. (See Mammon, below). No doubt my distaste is reinforced by my relative ineptitude in those areas.

"Do not separate yourself from the community" has a connection with the interest I have in family history. A first step in reaching out to the community, perhaps, is being clear who you are in your family setting.

"If I am not for myself . . . " etc. has found a strong resonance in our days. Irma felt the need for it.

When I was 6 or 8, if I was sent to the delicatessen on our block and came back with the wrong change and was sure I had not lost it on the way, my mother would make me go back to say 'you gave me the wrong change.' How I hated that. I have always been willing to give up my rights rather than endure the pain of claiming them.

My uncle Max Keane always made himself felt. He dressed with care, conducted himself with obvious self respect. He invariably sent food back to the kitchen in a restaurant—it was a predictable tic—but it is said that he always did so in so soothing a manner that the waitress and the kitchen staff never felt it as a put-down.

Training in assertiveness has been I think a feature of the '80s. On an Elderhostel trip, there were several people (a husband and wife otherwise quite interesting, and one or two more) who behaved in a conspicuously ugly manner. Often this behavior was triggered by fairly legitimate claims. It turned out that they had taken training courses in 'assertiveness', but apparently they had taken the elementary course in "If I am not for myself, who will be" and had not yet completed the lessons in how to do it with politeness, tact, and a sense of humor. And they had clearly not taken the intermediate course in "If I am only for myself, what am I."

Although this gnomic passage rings for us, the original commentary is very flat and lacking in energy, at least in Rodkinson's translation, which is not, I believe, highly regarded but I suppose is accurate in showing that the early interpretation was merely: Once I die, there is nothing to add to my merits. Pah.

Whatever the early fathers really meant, our generation has given this passage our own meaning.

If someone says no to my friend G. about something she needs and has a right to have, it will not occur to her to say, I need it, or, I have a right to have it, or even, please make an exception, I have a real problem. This has surprised me because, as a former school teacher, she sometimes has a rather peremptory manner about certain things that she required, but generally she lacks assertiveness about her own real needs where it is properly called for. Often I can effectively coach her in advance: if they say Z you should say Y, (and that sometimes works). But I must admit I would not do that on my own behalf and I sometimes did not do so on Irma's. I would rather forego my rights. I am willing to suffer their lack—a touch not of masochism I think but of stoicism. I had a right to do that on my own account, but not on Irma's. Having become aware of that, I perhaps do a little better for G. than I did for Irma.

11/7/95

Truth

I have a specially sensitive reaction to lying. It is not that I think lying is worse than say murder, but murder I simply reject, while lying is actively offensive to me.

My wife, Irma (and my daughter, Jan), have commented on my particular hatred for liars.

In the political world, I remember with special discomfort certain individuals—an assistant to a Vice President, for example, who wanted a photo opportunity of the V.P. waving goodbye to a trainload of ghetto kids (in Los Angeles, I think) going off for a summer vacation in unused barracks at an Army Camp (Fort Ord, I think). That this project used empty barracks, excess basketball courts and other playing fields was a valid argument for it. That it was psychologically unsound to put these kids down in the midst of men with guns and military security and who (probably) resented their presence, their freedom, and expectable minor depredations, and physically unsound because the barracks had been put out of service and were not readily rehabilitated on short notice, these were valid arguments against it. The V.P.'s aide told the Army (falsely) that the Office of Economic Opportunity had approved it; told the Mayor and the Community Action Organization (falsely) that both OEO and the Army had approved it. By running these lies fast enough around the circle, he got the plan approved (over my doubts) and the V.P. got his photo opportunity. In politics, that was probably considered a clever operation worth a promotion. Because it rested on a structure of lies (even though, by lying fast enough, the VP's aide made it all seem to come true), it has always rankled for me. There are many such examples.[32]

Perhaps closely allied to my special hatred of lying is my hatred of hypocrisy—the bitterly unchristian behavior of the "Christian Right"—the viciously homophobic themes of Senator McCarthy and his minions.

Perhaps a reason for this special hatred is an awareness that I am not likely to murder but could very easily lie. Indeed, Irma used to say I was a pathological liar. I enjoyed saying things that were not so, to explore how plausible I could make them seem, to explore whether there was a possible other side to an argument, to explore what arguments could be advanced by an opponent. This insight into the techniques of falsehood may have improved my judgment. I did not, however, deliberately mislead. If asked I would promptly acknowledge that what I said was not true. If not asked but I saw that a falsehood was being launched, I would volunteer a correction.

Irma used to say that it was easy to tell when I was lying. If I said something that seemed quite plausible, I was lying. If I said something that seemed quite unbelievable, trust me—it is true. [Example—perhaps: That there are animal species in which the males carry the eggs to term and nurture the young—or that there are birds that can fly upside down—if you are unprepared to believe that—believe it—I didn't make that up.]

My grandmother Freide Leah once made a visit (from Minsk or from Kharkov) to Vienna.[33] She was accompanied, I believe, by a daughter, and her purpose was to visit her brother-in-law Anshel (=Anselm) and sister-in-law Miriam, who were in Austria under an assumed name, perhaps because of a suspected or real connection with an anarchist plot to assassinate the Tsar.[34]

In Vienna, she said on her return, there are some very tall buildings. (The spire of St. Stephen's Church was 135 meters high—that is perhaps the height of a 35 story building). There is a church spire, she said, the height of a 15 story building. Imagine.

Her daughter said, Mama, you know that spire is more than twice that height. Freide Leah said, Yes, I know it, and you know it, but do I want to be taken for a liar?

Reb Itzikl, the Holy Seer of Lublin (Yaakov-Yitzhak ben Meitel? 1745-1815) said people flocked to him *because* he did not understand why they come. He apparently regretted the drain on his energies. A misnaged (enemy of the Hsidim), Reb Azriel Hurwitz, Der Eizener Kop (the Mind of Steel) in what was, although he was a misnaged, a friendly conversation, said to Reb Itzikl, People call you Tzaddik (a Just Man, an ideal of moral, social, religious perfection). Yet both you and I know that you are not. When you admit publicly that you are not, the people flock to you all the more because they admire your humility. So why don't you tell them that you are indeed, a true Tzaddik and people will resent your vanity and leave you alone. The Seer refused. "I agree with you that I am *not* a Tzaddik. But I am not a liar either.[35]

Two Jews, businessmen, met at the railroad station in Minsk. They chat. How are things, Reb Yankl? How are things, Reb Dovid? How should they be? You live and you work hard. Where are you going, Reb Yankl? I am going to Pinsk to see how is the lumber market there.

Reb Dovid looks at Reb Yankl and smiles. Yankl says, What are you smiling about, Reb Dovid? Dovid says, Why do people always lie? Yankl says, Lie? What lie? Have I ever lied to you? Dovid says, Come, come, Reb Yankl. You purposely said you were going to Pinsk about lumber so that I would think you were going to Kiev about wheat. But I happen to know that you really are going to Pinsk about lumber, so why do you lie to me?

8/30/86

My friend, Jack Karro, once cashed a government salary check at a bank, along with several other transactions. The teller gave him the money and by mistake also gave back the check with the bank's stamp on it. When Jack got home, he realized what had happened and went back to the bank to return the check. Although it was now after hours, Jack pounded on the door and finally persuaded the unwilling guard to let him in. The teller (who, under the rules then, could not leave until she balanced her account) saw the check, screamed, My out!, and kissed him.

Jack then went home and studied whether there was a way he could have kept the money and still benefited from having the check. When he satisfied himself that he had found a way to do so, he felt good because otherwise he would have had no merit in having returned the check.

11/7/95

My hatred for lying carries me into difficulties with bureaucracies. I am reluctant to answer form questions with inaccurate answers even though the drafter has not allowed for alternatives that are present, or though slightly fudged answers would be welcome.

In the 1940s, when I asked for advance induction and reported to the induction center, we were told to strip for medical examination and then told to sign and turn in a card acknowledging receipt of one complete uniform—underwear, socks, shirt, pants, jacket, boots, cap. I refused because I had not received a uniform. I think the young non-com had never encountered this problem and mentally ran through what he could do to me, but I was still a civilian, although a naked one. Somehow, I faced him down. In the end, I was rejected by the medical examiners and never got the uniform I was supposed to have acknowledged receiving.

I am reminded—l'havdl, that is, respecting the differences between us—of Richard Feynman's encounter with Selective Service. He was rejected on psychiatric grounds because he gave scrupulously accurate answers to a psychiatrist—bureaucrat.[36]

Although I hate liars and hate lying, I do not always feel compelled to volunteer the truth. I sometimes make accurate statements, which make it unnecessary to volunteer.

Two Russians and a Jew were once arrested for gambling at cards. Brought before a Judge, the Russians each swore that he had not been playing. Under Russian law, their oaths sufficed to clear them. The Jew said, Your Honor, so with whom am I supposed to have been playing?

This is, as an ethnic joke, a violation of modern niceties. But I think the Jew's evasion is not uncharacteristic. [I acknowledge that my willingness to duck may not be wholly consistent with my unwillingness to lie].

As to the Russians' false statements, I am sure that, at least in the Communist era, this lying is also characteristic. I have met it many times in many contexts.

A friend, Ken Adelman, and I were twice thrown out of Patrice Lumumba University dormitories near Moscow by the "Kommandants", door guards, although invited by Third World students. The Third World students turned and fled.

Meeting a Russian student, we were assured with a laugh that *he* as a Russian, would take us to *his* dorm, but we were barred again. This time at least, the student didn't flee. I asked, Couldn't we just sit in the lounge and talk? No. Could I just go to the men's room? No. I protested that I come from America where anyone can walk into a University building freely.—Well, it is the same here, but of course you have to get permission.—How do I get permission?—Do you have passport identification? (He plausibly assumed I did not, because when a foreigner checks into a hotel, his passport is sequestered, but to his astonishment, I did have my passport because I had already checked out in anticipation of leaving very early in the morning.) He then consulted an older woman guard and returned and said, yes, well you can get permission. You go to the University office about 20 miles the *other* side of Moscow, here is the address, on the second floor there is an office. They will give you permission.

We walked outside in the cold November weather with our crest-fallen Russian acquaintance. I asked whether there wasn't somewhere where we could sit down indoors, where we could be warm, perhaps have a cup of tea, and continue our conversation. Oh yes, there is a fine student cafeteria. So we walked there, saw through the large glass windows a brightly lit hall with students walking back and forth, carrying trays, seated, drinking tea, eating cake, playing chess. There it is, said the Russian student. "But as you can see, it is closed."

Because my wife was not well and was alone in the hotel, I then went back to the hotel, but my friend stayed and wound up in the dormitory late at night with a crowd of drinking Russians, thus proving his capacity for negotiation, which he later displayed as Reagan's Chief of Disarmament.

In Kiev, I told our Intourist guide we wanted to go to Babi Yar. Nevozmoshne, not possible, it is far, it is complicated. The driver does not know how to get there.

We persisted. They took us there. It turned out to be a simple, short, straight-forward drive. Of course, they knew that and had simply tried to respect the party line that Babi Yar was to be played down.[37] (And did not happen to Jews: If a memorial in Hebrew or Yiddish was placed there, it was promptly removed).

In Kiev, also, we were accosted surreptitiously by Jews who begged for materials for underground study of Hebrew, a forbidden activity (as Ukrainian study had been not long before). "Get us 'elef milim' ('A Thousand Words', a Hebrew primer) and we will make photo copies." We later met with the head of language study for Ukraine. He told us that every Ukrainian student learns at least three languages: Russian "of course"; Ukrainian "of course" (the 'of course' was a lie in view of the recent history of suppression of Ukrainian); and a third language of his choice, English, Chinese, Swahili, "whatever he chooses." Hebrew? Yiddish? "Of course, if he *chooses*, but *no* one chooses."

After protesting against being excluded from visiting universities in Moscow and Kiev, our group (an American government group studying education systems) was assured we would visit the University in Leningrad.

Sure enough, our bus took us to the University. We were met at the gate by the Rector, who led us through throngs of busy students to his office, locked the door, offered us tea, gave us a fine history of the University. We said, Thank you. Very nice. But we wanted to meet students and see classes in operation. "Oh! If I had *only* known. But unfortunately, today, the University is closed."

A friend of mine has commented on these stories and many more of similar pattern, that Russians don't really *lie*. It is not a lie when you know that they know that you know that they are lying.

12/11/95

Truth in the law

As a lawyer, I am deeply troubled by the fact that court decisions of important issues are rendered on false sets of facts. Every lawyer is bound to recognize this, yet there is no general systematic acknowledgment of this fact nor of its consequences.

Karl Llewellyn, for example, seems to agree that the facts are distorted,[38] yet thinks that is not important. If I understand him, I disagree. I think he means that *his* intuition is so keen that *he* gets the real facts in spite of the distortions.

2/8/97

There are appropriate ways to correct at least some of this distortion[39], but I have found very little professional interest in doing so.

12/11/95

A major reason that cases are decided on false sets of facts is that legal processes progressively distort and suppress truth. There is a motion to dismiss: we must take as fact any allegation of the pleading and indeed any possible favorable circumstance consistent with the pleading.

A jury has rendered a verdict: if there is evidence that could support the verdict, we must take it as true.

There is an appeal: We must take as true every possible state of facts that could support the decision below.

By the time a case gets to the Supreme Court, the Court has before it a tissue of non-facts that are 'the facts of the case.'

I have seen this happen in every case I have been close to, and I have been very upset by it. I understand why the system works that way, and at every step it can be justified, but the ultimate result is that principles are decided on the basis of 'facts' that are not facts.

This is especially harmful when new institutions and new bodies of law are being created: alien property law, community action, grants, affirmative action.[40]

Add to this the additional distortions caused by advocates who may be skilled in advocacy but do not know the facts . . . [41] and by advocates who know the facts and misrepresent them . . . and by legal presumptions counter to truth . . . The law, as Dickens' spokesman, Mr. Bumble in Oliver Twist, said, is a ass.

1/18/98

Anyone who uses words thoughtfully knows that every word you use carries implications and suggestions that you don't intend and that every effort to make your expression more accurate and eliminate the unintended will also defeat some aspect of accuracy.

A trial or legal argument is primarily a process for describing facts in words. An initial distortion in all legal matters is this inherent distortion from the use of words, multiplied by the uncertain variety of word users—ignorant or sophisticated—careful or careless—and multiplied again by the artificial character of the occasion.

"It all depends on what the meaning of the word is is".

Simenon[42] shows another aspect of this in Maigret aux Assizes (Maigret in Criminal Court):

"Wasn't everything distorted? Not by any fault of the judges, the jury, the witnesses, nor of the statute or the rules of procedure, but because human beings were suddenly summed up, so to speak, in a few words, in a few sentences . . . "

"Learned historians, [Maigret said], devote their lives to studying an historical figure on whom books have already been written. They scurry from library to library, they scour the archives, they look for the slightest connections in order to get at just a bit more of the truth . . . For fifty years and more, they have studied Stendhal to understand a bit better his character . . . "

"But when a crime is committed, almost always by someone out of line—that is to say less easy to understand than the man in the street, I get weeks, perhaps only days to interrogate ten, twenty, fifty people wholly unknown to me up till then and to find the truth . . . . The case is penciled in, in a few quick strokes, the actors are no more than sketches if not frankly caricatures . . . . "

8/4/97

Dichtung und Wahrheit

A bright young man was hired by my agency in the contract section. His work, to his shock and my surprise, was found unsatisfactory. To save his job, he was transferred to my section (grants). I found his work competent and he later went on to a satisfying career in another agency. When I took him on, I told him why I thought he had not worked out in the contract section. A valued asset in government contract work is the ability to lie shamelessly, and, if caught, move on without embarrassment. A contract officer often tells a bidder or contractor, this provision, or this interpretation, is required by law. If you know enough to say No, it's not, or even enough to say, Show me, he moves on as though he never said it. My new young assistant respected truth and simply did not have the talent to lie and move on.

I once negotiated a contract with the government of Guatemala, which was represented by a prominent American lawyer active in Guatemalan affairs and by Guatemalan advisors. The Guatemalans told me that a certain clause they wanted in the contract was required by the Guatemalan Constitution. I got out the text of their Constitution and read out a provision that said the contrary. The negotiation proceeded as though that clause had never been mentioned. After the contract was signed, the American lawyer asked me where I had studied Guatemalan law. I never had, of course, but Spanish is not a difficult language.

As acting head of the Office of Alien Property, I asked the Swiss for certain information about corporate interests held through Swiss corporations. The Swiss economic attaché came to see me and explained that his government wished to cooperate but, of course, I would understand that to supply this information would violate the Swiss Constitution. I replied that of course I understood and respected his difficulty. And of course, he would understand that, lacking the information I had asked for, I would have to conclude that the interests were German. The next day, the attaché brought me answers to my questions. I don't say that the answers were accurate, but, at the least, I had amended the Swiss Constitution overnight.

6/9/97

Yiddish faking

Do you know what a nature faker is? He tells you that that's an ichneumon fly because he knows you won't know and are not going to check on him.

There are also Yiddish fakers. The Jews who gave the lexicographer Eric Partridge absurd explanations of the origins of words like Kibosh. Partridge doesn't know. Doesn't know how to check. Believes them and prints their story—after all, they are Jewish.

Kabash in Hebrew means to subdue (and in other ways to down). Is that not the origin of to put the kibosh on? Some Yiddishist let Partridge and other lexicographers believe that kibosh[43] in Yiddish means 18 pence. How silly can you get. But what does Partridge know. Yes, ki *could* represent chai (=18). But how would bosh mean pence and how would 18 pence mean to suppress.

Even Leo Rosten, believing that the card game 'pisha-paysha'[44] comes from 'Pitch and Patience' or 'Peace and Patience'—ridiculous. Rosten could have thought about it, he had background enough and was backed up by my friend Bruno Schachner, but he was writing a pot-boiler. The game is like Go Fish. In Hebrew, Pish poosh means a search. Pash paysh means to search. Pisha paysha is obviously a variant of that Hebrew and it is descriptive. If there is a game called Pitch and Patience—a silly name on its face, is it not an English corruption of the Hebrew, not the other way around?

I do not know but suspect that a 'Festival of Regrets' discussed in a profile of Wendy Wasserstein may be a similar piece of imagination. I am talking about the profile, I have not read the Wasserstein piece referred to. That I don't know about this Festival proves nothing, but it has the smell: if the idea comes from Wasserstein, then it's not exactly faking, she is a poet and is entitled to her poetry but the profile swallowed it as truth.[45]

8/4/97

Success in practice?

Certain qualities that make for success in a law practice are not in my quiver. I do not have a taste for the things that make money nor an ability to do them.[46]

I had four years of experience as a litigation supervisor at the National Labor Relations Board. Labor practice can be financially rewarding. I never practiced in the labor field.

When I left the Office of Alien Property as General Counsel, there were large fees to be earned by lawyers in matters of seized or frozen foreign assets. My knowledge of the field and my paper credentials were certainly impressive but, with one exception, none of the major business came to me, and that exception I gave up: A foreign nation asked me to represent its interests in corporate matters in the United States, not including those I had been personally involved in. The incoming Republican Attorney General said that while it was not a violation of the conflict of interest laws for me to accept the retainer, he would *prefer* that I not accept it because I had met the representatives of the country involved when I was a government official. The client's representatives angrily replied that the Attorney General could not dictate their choice of counsel. I advised them, however, that it was not in their interest to be represented by a lawyer whom the United States did not want to be their representative. This was not only a substantial piece of individual business but could have been the basis for the creation of a major law firm.

Soon after, another nation asked me to represent it in a particular matter. Obviously, I had met the representatives of that nation also when I was a government official. No one objected. I think it fair to infer that the objection in the first case rested on no principle. In the case of the Attorney General, it reflected a desire to hurt Democrats, which I saw in other actions as well (the unwarranted prosecution of a former Assistant Attorney General, for example; the wholesale discharge of many of the Alien Property staff, followed by a request to come back when the positions could not be filled by young ambitious Republicans who preferred jobs in agencies that were growing, not winding down like the post-war Alien Property office). On the part of the staff, I think it reflected a small touch of envy, a strong dash of naïve holier-than-thouness, and perhaps some touch of desire to get along with the new Administration. (A friend, perhaps better informed than I, attributes the wholesale discharge to compliance with the anti-Semitism of an influential Senator. I believe my explanation is at least part of the motivation).

In the area of grant law, where my knowledge of the field and recognized credentials are outstanding, I have spent most of my private professional life persuading clients that they don't need me. Of course, that is partly, but not entirely, a reflection of my age. I no longer welcome confrontations. Perhaps I never did, but in the past I was at least quite willing to be confrontational when it was called for.

As a matter of personality, I have no bluff, no self-assurance, no ability to claim and to demand more than is justified. These characteristics sometimes help success in law practice more than knowledge and ability.

3/8/95

Mammon

It is said often by non-Jews that Jews are money-motivated. I know this is not true in my own life and my family's.

Irma and I were agreed from the beginning that in our career choices, mostly choices of my career, we would choose the path of satisfaction in our work, not money return. Had we opted for money, I do not know that the choice would have been successful: I am not gifted in making money. But we chose in any case to try, to the extent that we had a choice, for work that was satisfying, and in part, publicly worthwhile.

We spent some 20 years working on the TMT bankruptcy case. We entered that work knowing that we would have to subsidize it; that, while we expected some remuneration at the end, it was likely to be, and it proved to be, inadequate for the time spent, for the quality of our work, for the risks we undertook, and for the success achieved. I had investigated the new form of transportation pioneered by the company (roll-on-roll-off) and had informed some investors that I believed the idea sound. I had not explored the possibility that the company would be more guided by stock manipulation than by its sound business prospects. When the company failed, we pursued this work because of the challenge, of the opportunity for learning new skills and for creativeness, and because we were stubborn, or I was, and because of a sense of obligation.[47]

In our personal lives, we were content to spend little for rent, to live in furnished rooms, to sleep on the floor when in an unfurnished apartment. We spent nothing on ostentation, little on clothing, little on entertainment, somewhat more on food of good quality, for Irma was an excellent cook. Our priority was books and, when we had children, their education.

In both the Kahn and Mason families, there was some financial success,[48] but it was not what we took pride in. Indeed, for most of my life, until I started writing family history, I mistakenly believed our family was poor.

My socialist uncle Gabe, in his autobiography writes admiringly of my father's entrepreneurial success,[49] but that was not what I admired my father for.

The pervading motivation in the Mason family has been Mason communism: from each according to his abilities, to each according to his needs.

Camp Greylock for Boys, I believe, was a financial success, but an important motivation pervading the project was that it afforded opportunities to use skills, and opportunities for nepotism, and a love of camping on the part of my uncles, especially George and Gabe.

My uncle George, a Master Forester, built it, and guided the woodsiness of the camp program. My uncle Gabe, a school principal, had a major part in supervising the educational program. Later, they settled on George as Director of the younger camp, Gabe of the older. Lou and Herman ran business aspects of the camp. Gabe's wife, Ricca, played the piano with musical skill and popular verve. Lou and George's wives, Fan and Esther, helped in business management. My father chose the medical and nursing staff and visited them as his time permitted. My aunt Rebecca ran the household (visitors' housing, camp laundry, seamstress). My cousin Anita ran the kitchen (as she did at Gabe's School). My mother was 'camp mother' for the youngest group. The family's boys all went to camp, before the season, as campers during the season, and after the season. So far as I know, they did not pay. Every year the clan gathered for a family picture with my grandparents (when they were alive) on the lawn at the top of the hill.[50]

The girls camp was not a financial success, but only a place of love. We overpaid on counselors' salaries, insisted on luxury quality of food. When Irma and I took over the management, we subsidized it to an extent greater than our own annual income at the time. We gave it up because of that, and because of the conflict with our beginning law practice. I was negotiating a very difficult family dispute and had drafted a set of papers to reflect our proposal and had them signed by our side. They were of course not to be delivered except in exchange for corresponding papers from the other side.

I used to go up to camp, an 8 hour car trip, every weekend and back every Sunday or Monday. When I got to the office on Monday my secretary told me that Miss X (the very tough lawyer for the other side) had phoned to ask whether the papers were ready and had sent a messenger for them. "Since she seemed to know all about them, I gave them to her." (This of course gave her a strong negotiating advantage.) As I was feeling the floor sink under me, Irma called from camp.

The second cook was running after the chef with a meat cleaver. What should I do? I said, What can I tell you? I am 300 miles away. Call the sheriff. Irma felt that I lacked concern.

I tell this story primarily to explain the conflict between our law practice and running a camp. My daughter likes it because she feels it also reflects the traditional difference between Venus and Mars sharpened by a crisis at both ends.

I had bought out in installments the interests of my uncle Herman and of my mother (represented by the three children, Bryna, and Irv, as well as myself). I have no doubt that if I had been unable to pay, payment would have been forgiven or deferred.

In previous generations, my ancestors, Ritevsky and Mosesson, had a chain of 'galanterie'[51] businesses, in which each new son or son-in-law was set up: my grandfather Aaron first in Minsk, later in Kharkov. My greatuncle Solomon in Warsaw (I don't know that he was set up by the family, but I assume it). My uncle Isidor was apprenticed to his uncle Solomon, and so on.

My mother's brother Maxwell Keane (he ersified the family name Kahn) was a born salesman. He lived a yo-yo life: our richest uncle, then broke. When he was broke, my mother took into our home Max, his wife Emmy, and son Bob. My father got Max work selling stock in a chain of drug stores (Neve Drugs, on alternate corners down Manhattan's spine) created by Pop and (probably more important) his partner Ben Lurie, and selling stock to physicians in the hospitals organized by Pop and Lurie. My mother got Bob started in his career with a job with Jo Lo Baking Supplies, owned by Joe Lowe, father of a camper at the girls camp.

When a hospital was organized in the Bronx, it was a 'non-profit', like many such, in the Pickwickian sense that the 'profits' were disguised as benefits to insiders. Pop was offered the position of head of a department. I think it was the cardiology department, but it might have been the obstetrics department. Pop was a family practitioner but had taken post-graduate work in cardiology—I suspect because he had misgivings about his heart or, more probably, my mother's. He found that it was expected that he make a sizable contribution to the hospital, in exchange for which he would be able to determine which doctors could practice there and which patients would be admitted, a power that would enable him very quickly to recoup his contribution. I remember his mulling over this with my mother. Possibly, he did not have the money, but probably he could have borrowed it. He was, however, offended by this arrangement and turned it down. He then created the Royal Hospital on a new and opposed principle: an 'open' hospital in which any appropriately licensed and certified physician could bring his patients, the first of three such hospitals. This was very successful and produced what I believe (with my prejudiced viewpoint) was the best hospital in New York. Little by little, Medicaid and Medicare rules and, especially, City rules established by Professor Ray Trussel of Columbia P. & S. (a theorist in hospital management, inefficient in hospital practice as demonstrated later, in my biased view, when he headed Beth Israel) forced the open hospital to approach the organization of the 'non-profit' hospitals my father had rebelled against. Ultimately, the pressures of bad regulation led us, after my father died and my brother Irv was Director of the Royal (Ben Lurie of Kew Gardens) to close rather than comply. New York is the poorer for it.

I was President of the Hospital Laundry Service. Lurie's wife's nephew, Leo Katzen, was operating head of the Laundry Service. Lurie's brother-in-law Jack Katzen was accountant for the Hospitals and the Laundry Service.

Irma's brother Bob needed a job. We got him a job working for our Hospital Laundry Service, and later set him up in business for himself as a Diaper Service. This took money, of which we had little, plus our connections with the industry. My mother-in-law, Anne Slosberg, was grateful and tried to repay us with stock that had become worthless in the 1929 stock market crash and remained so. Of course, she hoped it would recover and that we would benefit.

A related topic: we have never been inclined to assert rights we believed we had. My father used to say: I would rather have a partner I know is a crook than a partner I don't know is a crook[52]. Bryna, Irv, and I, have tolerated many overreachings. We do not push our rights. I believe Irma was seriously mistreated by George Washington University Hospital with physical damage to her health, but neither Irma nor I cared to press the issue beyond informing Dr. Silver for his benefit and that of other patients.

Irma used to say of my father and me, 'anything for peace'. Rae also said this of Morris.

I think my uncle George was an exception to this attitude. I have known him to speak directly and effectively against unfair treatment. I think in this he took after his mother, Freide Leah.[53]

7/25/96

Missed Manners

I am socially inept. I think this ineptitude is specifically mine rather than in the family. Is there anything I could have done or my family could have done to make me grow up less gauche? I don't know. Send me to finishing school.

4/8/95

Cognitive Dissonance—Saying No

One of my vices is finding and holding onto bad reasons to not do what I know I am not going to do, anyway. It is hard to give clear examples but here are some examples that are real but a little caricaturish. If a solicitor calls me for a charity that I do not intend to contribute to, I will note things about his call that I do not like, as though they were reasons not to contribute. But I know I do not intend to contribute in any case. He should not be calling at this hour. I do not like the standard take-you-in pitch, "And how are you today?", I don't like his using my first name. I don't like his grammar. I never pledge in advance; when the time comes, I either contribute or I don't. Many charities open their solicitations by saying that I have pledged. I have an exaggerated resentment of that misrepresentation. All of this is absurd. I have no need to contribute to charities I have not chosen. Why do I turn these complaints into pseudo-reasons for not contributing. Is there a half-conviction that one must contribute if asked.

Similarly calls by stockbrokers. I know I don't buy stock from a broker who calls me blind, but I note and recall my petty resentments, such as the first name, or the Lehman Brothers ploy: 'please hold for Mr. Jones, Vice-President of Lehman Bros.', intended to impress. I would hang up, but since I was director of some sizable companies and practicing in the securities field there is the off chance that I need to take the call. I once represented a broker-dealer whose staff made calls all day to sell stock. I'm not sure they called strangers, they were supposed not to do so, but perhaps they did. I think they tended rather to call people with whom they had some small prior connection.

12/31/94

Charity

I receive many solicitations for charitable contributions that I reject. Some seem to me phony. Some I don't approve. Some, I am aware, or suspect, of excessive personal luxury to officers. But many seem to have merit. Still, I don't want to dribble contributions to every non-objectional charity. Why not? Wouldn't this be a better world if I did or if everyone did? I have friends who tithe—make a point of contributing one-tenth of their income. My own contributions are much less. I have settled on certain charities and regularly send them each year what I sent last year, occasionally making an adjustment for inflation. U.J.A., S.O.M.E., University Settlement, J.N.F. (memorial trees as occasion presents). When I reject a request, I usually feel some guilt. And look for something in the solicitation I object to: they spelled my name wrong, they call me by my first name, they addressed Mr. and Mrs. long after Irma died, they pretend falsely that I contributed to them in the past or had requested their information or had made a pledge. These criticisms are captious and I know they are. I am aware that if the solicitation had not had contained these flaws, I was not going to contribute anyway. But I persist in thinking these objections, I suppose because it slightly eases the pain of refusing. Jewish Social Service, Simon

Wiesenthal Center, Cancer Society, Heart Association, Multiple Sclerosis, Birth Defects—how can I refuse? Columbia Law School: here and in Hebrew Home for the Aged, I have offered services but not money. My prejudices are hard to justify. American Red Cross—well, there I have some long standing resentments: they effectively took sides in labor disputes in the '30s by refusing, in pretended 'neutrality', emergency aid to striking workers, and when Israel was attacked, they refused to give or sell or lend certain medical supplies of which they had a practical monopoly (my sister Bryna, as a Hadassah officer had the job of trying to obtain these supplies). [54]

5/5/00

The International Red Cross has long refused to admit the Mogen Dovid Adom, Red Star of David, on the hypocritical ground that it did not use the Red Cross symbol, although it did not hesitate to admit the Muslim Red Crescent. Recently (2000) the American Red Cross, to its credit, has urged the International Red Cross to (at least) grand-father the Mogen Dovid Adom. Emil Sandstrom, Swedish President of the International Red Cross about 1950, once raised his glass at a reception at our house in Alexandria with the toast, "Next year in Jerusalem", but the IRC still will not recognize Israel.

5/29/95

There is a company that appears to be staffed by handicapped people. It sells, at high prices, some common items by telephone. The opening declaration is: This is not a charity (I am a handicapped person). In fact it is not a charity. It is a profit making venture for its sponsors. I believe, however, that the opening statement: This is not a charity, has the effect for many hearers, and I think the effect is intended, of being understood as: This is a charity but see how brave we are that we do not ask you to deal with us as a charity. I have received calls from them and have turned them down with a touch of guilt for saying no.

The SEC requires certain disclaimers. Writers of registration statements make these disclaimers but have a degree of hope (which is somewhat justified) that the semi-sophisticate reading them will say, Of course, they have to say that, but it is reasonable to think the contrary:

> No approval is to be implied . . .
>
> Past history is no guide to future income . . .

SEC wants the disclaimer to be believed. The registrant wants the reader to assume a wink.

But, see the prospectus for Berkshire Hathaway B. It has the usual required disclaimer along with the unusual declaration: "Warren Buffet . . . and Charles Mayer want you to know the following (and urge you to ignore anyone telling you that these statements are boiler plate or unimportant) . . . "[55]

2/20/95

There are instructions that are given with the expectation and intent that they not be followed.

Fair Share

When I was a member of the Stephen Wise Free Synagogue, I was appointed to the Fair Share Committee. This was an activity

I did not approve, but in accordance with my view that we must try things, I did it once.

The Synagogue was Free in two senses. Stephen Wise did not want a synagogue where he was told what he could preach, so he left his fine pulpit at Emanuel and created a new one across the park where the rabbi (that is, himself) was free to preach what the rabbi (that is, himself) thought right. It was also free in that seats were not sold. A member could attend and pay no fixed sum but what his heart told him was his fair share.

Now many of us, facing so open-ended a choice, welcome a hint, a suggestion, a comparison. When tipping a waiter, we would feel very lost if someone had not told us that 15% is very usual, not required but a good way to start thinking. More, if service is very good, or more, if drinks have been ordered. Less, theoretically, if service has been poor, but rarely does anyone venture to rate service so sternly. But start with figuring 10% plus half of 10%, rounded up.   If we who are not accustomed to cruises go on a cruise, we do not resent, we welcome a suggestion about what are customary tips to whom.   When we give Christmas gifts to the Irene staff, I would be pleased if some other tenant or even a manager would tell me whether what I give is unusually high or, more likely, unusually low. (But those I have asked tell me 'whatever you feel is right'. That is not helpful).

So the members of the Free Synagogue could well be glad to have a suggestion of what others are giving for membership: $10, $100, $1000, $10,000? 10% of their annual income? The Fair Share Committee, by giving such hints, can serve a useful and friendly purpose. Jewish organizations are well-known for sometimes rough pressure, shaming tactics in money-raising. This has a long tradition behind it. Itinerant preachers after giving a sermon, and representatives of good religious causes, went from door to door asking for gifts. Jokes abound on the clever and nasty things they are said to have said to someone who did not give or did not give enough.

An itinerant preacher (a magid), after preaching on Saturday went house to house on Sunday, as the custom was, to ask for gifts. When a rich man (a nogid, a gvir) turned him down, he said, People wonder why, when a dog chases a pig, he goes for the pig's ear. I can tell you. The Talmud tells us there is no one as rich as a pig and no one as poor as a dog. [Is that true? Is that in the Talmud? I don't know, but it is possible. There is no index.] When the dog chases the pig, he goes for his ear, so he can say to him, "Since you are so rich, why are you such a pig?"   I don't think these stories are very realistic, but there are many of them. I think they reflect a joy in a clever put-down of the rich, and a sense that it was normal to raise money by rough pressure, and that a poor man raising money was privileged. Zangwill's character The Shnorer (beggar) is typical of this. So is also the story about the beggar who insisted on seeing Rothschild personally about his business. When Rothschild found he had come for a gift, he angrily said, For that, did you have to see me personally; any one of my Secretaries could have taken care of it. The beggar said, Reb Anshel, no doubt you know all about business. Certainly more than I. But when it comes to begging, don't *you* try to teach *me*.

The instructions of the Fair Share Committee were to avoid pressure. We were only to help people make their own decision by giving them indications of what others were doing. This was sound and valid. I am sure, however, that if the committee did not come back with an increase in the contributions, we would be considered to have done a disappointing job.

When I was a Tammany Precinct Captain in Stevenson's second election campaign, or thereabouts, I was given a lump sum of money—maybe $200—I don't remember how much. It was called walking-around money. No accounting would be asked for. If money was left over, of course, we could keep it. Of course, we were not to buy votes. If a voter was disabled or for any reason had difficulty getting to the polls, we could hire a taxi. But I had no such voters. I bought no votes. I needed no taxis. I did not want to receive payment for being a precinct captain. I brought the money back after the election. Our District Leader (Congressman Teller) looked at me with contempt. He rightly saw that I did not have the making of a Tammany precinct captain. He knew that I should have known that the instructions I had been given were not intended to be followed.

When a party fund-raising dinner is held, government employees must not be pressured to contribute. But government supervisors were often given lists and tickets and instructed not to pressure, 'but as an accommodation', to make tickets available. I did not buy (except perhaps once because of my usual principle—see what it's like, once), but I am sure that supervisors generally understood that do not pressure did not mean, let your employees feel unpressured. This is why I think government employees unions are wrong to oppose the Hatch Act that seeks to limit political activity.

Memory

I have a naturally good memory. My memory has also been trained, but so far as I can see the trained memory is quite separate from the untrained. I retain and can recall many details that others find surprising. Of course now in my 80s, recall is sometimes painfully slow. A stranger who shared a table at the Kennedy Center cafeteria asked whether we had heard the Israel Symphony when they were here recently. No. I wanted to add that I had heard them in Tel Aviv conducted by Milton Katims (in 1968). I knew quite well that the conductor then was a great violist, that in my view his skill as a violist impaired his conducting because he seemed to feel he had to indicate every hemidemisemi-quaver. He had been my classmate at Columbia College whom I knew better than most of my classmates. But I could not produce the name Milton Katims. Perhaps two days later I suddenly recalled. Oh, that was Milton Katims. A search light revolves in the skull, comes around and picks out what I am looking for. It may take time. But this is a problem of age. When I was younger it did not often take as long.

My mother, I think had a good memory. Her favorite poems were all ready at hand. Coming here as a girl she acquired a rich American English culture. My father, I think had a good memory. Coming here as a boy, he became a chemist, a pharmacist, a physician. My uncle Gabe had a notable memory. In talks on any subject, he could always adduce relevant long passages of poetry and historical facts. I suppose my good memory must be inherited. And of course we Jews have historically an oral tradition (not unique, but carried down perhaps more than most other peoples'). Pop had, in addition to a good memory, an ability to outguess exams. One morning he took a Regents exam in a subject he needed for his Pharmacist's certificate. On the way out, he noticed a posting of an exam that afternoon in Physiography. He had never studied Physiography and did not know what it was. (It is the part of geology that later interested me in the study of the surface shapes of the earth and their implications for underlying structures.) Since there was no fee and it would not hurt him to fail, he decided to stay and take the exam. He passed. A generation later, when I was full of my interest and skill in Physiography[56], Pop told me how he too had an A in Physiography.

In addition to natural memory, there is some trained memory. When I was 6, my mother taught me long narrative poems (like the One Hoss Shay and like The Courting by—(blockage)—James Whitcomb Riley—I think. ("You may want a span of horses for plowin' and all the rest, but when it comes to courtin', why, a single hoss is best"). My mother's method was to learn the first two lines, then the first four, then the first six and so on. People scolded her for overloading a child's brain, but she insisted memory does not get overloaded—it grows stronger with exercise. She may have been right.

Then both my father and my uncle Gabe took a course in memory training with a man named Berol. The method involved facilitating recall by somewhat artificial associations. Numbers were translated into letters and words by an easily learned consonant code. T (or D) was 1, N was 2, M 3, R four, L five (the El then cost 5¢), J 6 (or soft G or CH), K 7 (or hard C), F (or V) 8, P (or B) 9, S (or Z) zero. Vowels were free. Having this in hand, you could memorize telephone numbers. I was about 10 then, I think. I learned the system and could do set pieces: First—name all the presidents in order: Washington was # 1— just remember his (tricorn) haT. That's a real example. Now I'll make up some; Adam was Naked (# 2); Jefferson lived at Monticello (#3). Then—look once at every card in a shuffled deck of cards and call them off in order or (random access) name, say, the 29th card. Suppose the 29th card was a 7 of clubs: As you went through the cards, you will have made up a silly comment like: Why does IKE NAP at his CLUB. You won't forget that IKE(= 7) is NAP (=29) and it is club 7: Next, the Queen of Spades: The Queen of Spain was frightened by a MOUSE (=30) and so on. I am no longer quick enough to do this.

8/10/97

I remember directly, without aid, my father's telephone number at his laboratory on 125th Street. It was Morningside 1065. This was about 1915, when I was five. He later moved to 124th Street and I think kept the same number.

I remember, but because of a mnemonic, my Aunt Rose's telephone number when she lived near where they were building the George Washington Bridge—that was about 180th Street facing the Hudson River near the little lighthouse famous in a child's book. The number was Wadsworth 4174. I remember it because of the mnemonic, What's worth Red Car? R=4; d=1; hard c=7; r=4 again.

I remember, but because of a mnemonic plus an anecdote, the number Irma and I had when we lived on 115th Street west of Broadway (south side). It was Susquehanna 9-4720. This was about 1936. The mnemonic was Susie Perkins. (P=9, R=4, K=7, N=2, S=0). The anecdote is that we spent the summer in a rented place in an artists colony in New City (Ruth Reeve's place) where the number was something like New City 12. Pop wanted to call us there but asked for New City Susquehanna 9-4720. The operator said there was no such number. Pop said, what do you mean, no such number! Susie Perkins! Susie Perkins![57] The operator no doubt thought he was a nut.

For a period of several years, I used to write up accounts of our Friday lunch discussions. This was a discussion group that has met Fridays since about 1940 and has had and now has some distinguished members. I came as a guest of Sig Timberg's when I visited Washington 1950-1966, and became a member when I came back to Washington in 1966. My write-ups were initially an attempt to test my memory and perhaps to improve it by seeing how much I could recapture and to observe the methods of remembering. About methods, I note in particular that I do not recall all in one flow. That is in part why my writing accrues marginalia. It also became for a while an attempt to preserve a record of some discussions that I thought I would want to return to. After a while I largely discontinued it because it had served its first purpose of testing my memory, and the second of improving my memory, and perhaps the discussions had become less coherent without Oscar Gass, Ed Dale, Lou Krauthoff, Franz Oppenheimer.[58]

9/11/97

There is a special blessing to be said when something forgotten comes back to your memory: Baruch mazkir nishkahos Blessed be He who bringeth to remembrance things forgotten: Harkavy Dict. p. 153, said at recalling a thing forgotten.

3/19/97

For years, whenever I made oatmeal, I always thought of my friend Henry Hilken (my colleague at the Office of Alien Property and at the Brussels Inter-Allied Reparations Agency). I have no idea of what the connection of ideas was. We never made or ate oatmeal together. Perhaps once, very early, while making oatmeal I reminded myself that I was to telephone Henry, and it stuck for years.

When Henry died, I started thinking about Leon Ulman when I make oatmeal. Leon was another OAP colleague. Here the connection is of course a substitution of one colleague for another. I was very friendly with Henry. Leon, less so because he did not reciprocate overtures of friendship but he lived in the Irene as I did and we occasionally planned lunch together. I suppose that is why he rather than others became the substitute. Most of the time I would mix my oatmeal and think of Leon, then of Henry, or of Henry, then of Leon.

This seems to be a Lockean Association of Ideas. What is curious is that it stands alone as the only clear example I seem to have of such an association not readily attributable to a logical connection but apparently a chance connection that somehow became ingrained by repetition.

1/16/98

That and one more: Whenever I tie my shoes, I think of Norman and Sarah Frumkin. I have no idea what started this train of thought. Sarah was very kind to my wife Irma when Irma was sick. I remember her kindness with pleasure but what has tying my shoes got to do with it?

2/25/95

My natural memory does not run to people. I barely remember any of my college classmates beyond a small coterie or any of my law school classmates beyond a handful. My brother Irv, on the other hand, remembered not only his classmates, but mine, and that this one had gone on to do this, and that one had become that. Suppose I had developed an idea for some activity. Irv would say, well, your classmate X (whom I do not remember) now works for Y (which I did not know). He might be interested. I don't think I ever acted on these leads because I could not carry the burden of pretending to remember a classmate I did not remember, but I was always astonished that Irv knew these things. He remembered people. I remembered stuff in books.

2/24/95

Geography

Traditional Greek and Renaissance memory methods arranged things to be remembered spatially so that traversing an imaginary room or map you could recall them.

Geography is easier to remember than ideas or plans. One interesting indication of the efficacy of this principle is very familiar to seniors in what are called senior moments. If I need a pen, I will go to my study to get it. On the way, I may forget what I am going for, but my sense of geography will take me to the tray with pens and pencils, and if I then stand quietly in front of my desk, it will come back to me.

Trust your legs. Do not trust your hands but your legs.

Related to memory is a sense of geography. Irv had a strong sense of geography. If he ever drove anywhere once, thereafter he knew the road. I have a weaker sense of that kind. I am fairly good at knowing roads but not nearly as good as Irv was. On the other hand, walking in the woods, I have (or had) a strong sense of how to get back or (admitting the risk of impasses) how to take short cuts.

My brother-in-law, Bud, had a very strong memory of a different kind. Where I have a general sense that Congressman L. had an honorable record that he later besmirched by hypocritical partisan action or statements of a very offensive kind, Bud would have remembered just what they were, and just when, and just what the context was, what happened just before and just after. But often he had the weakness of that strength: he remembered so much, but could not leap over remembered detail for relevant detail.

2/24/95

Bud like Irv could give very accurate detailed road directions. I think that Irv's directions were more helpful to a driver who did not know the road. By hindsight, Bud's directions would be seen as accurate, but Irv's helped in advance.

When I tried to get colleagues at the National Labor Relations Board and my staff at the Office of Economic Opportunity and later at the Department of Health, Education, and Welfare Departmental Grant Appeals Board to make notes for an index on points decided in our decisions, most of the staff were unable to grasp the difference between recording correctly the facts they knew about the case and (what I sought) recording the facts that someone who did not know the case might be looking for.

My friend, RV, claimed that when he was in the French cavalry, he was taught how to give useful road directions. I don't know how it was taught, but it is a useful skill if it can be taught.

Our friend, Marvin Goidell, as a child, heard his father and his father's friends (Hungarian Jews in downtown New York) talking about their friends and the day's events and reminiscing. He absorbed it and retained it. Later, grown up, he could join in reminiscing as though he were of their cohort. "Do you remember old man so-and-so who had the drug store on the corner of Christie Street . . . " and was accepted, until someone would pull up short and say, Hey, Marvin, you weren't born then.

2/25/99

It is customary now-a-days to make lists of essential elements of our American culture (Bloom, e.g.). In my parent's generation, we didn't exactly make lists, but we had, in addition to spelling bees, general information contests (weekly, I think, at camp). These called for bits of information related to our being American: the names of the Presidents, Vice Presidents, States and their capitals, ball players, English poets, perhaps a few scientists. I usually did well in these because of my unpurposeful reading and good memory.

5/12/95

Why I am not a teacher

I am a very good teacher but lack some qualities of a good teacher: empathy, outgoingness, self-confidence. (Teaching is important in Jewish history: Talmud, Lamdan, Melamed, Lomed. What is a rabbi? a teacher.)

What qualities make me (in my estimation, but also in others') a good teacher? Patience. An ability to find principle behind practice without pedantry. A willingness to let beginners try their strengths—a lack of self seeking.

Then why am I not a teacher? Well, I have taught. I have taught nature study, woodcraft, wrestling, fencing, philosophy, law. I have carried out in-house training for the staffs of lawyers at the National Labor Relations Board, Office of Alien Property, Office of Economic Opportunity, Departmental Grant Appeals Board, at a law firm, and (on election law) at my political club. I have written a paper on brief writing that I am told was used as a text for in-house training at the SEC. That I have not settled as an academic is partly a result of accident and naïveté about academia, partly a result of possibly excessive humility, and partly a result of principle—a principle I shall explain later.

3/4/97

I have of course done a lot of teaching. I have tutored a cousin in math and in French when he was preparing for exams. I have tutored my brother in math and, later, friends of his in law school who were having difficulty. (Their later careers showed them to be amply skillful in lawyering. They did not need me for that—I got them over learning hurdles). I taught a course with Karl Llewellyn in legal argument. He taught oral argument. I taught written argument. I taught a survey course in Philosophy at City College. I taught a course in Grant Practice at the University of South Carolina. I have lectured extensively on alien property law and on grant law.

But why am I not a teacher by profession?

Philosophy

Why am I not a philosophy professor? A trivial reason and a deeper one. As an undergraduate I had taken doctoral level courses in Philosophy and had nearly the course credits for the degree but not the thesis, of course. I spent a graduate year in France on a fellowship from the Ministry of Public Instruction, studying (or supposed to be studying) Bergson with Bergson's principal disciple, Chevalier. I came back to New York in September and took it for granted that the Philosophy Department would offer me an instructorship or teaching assistantship. Irwin Edman said to me, my dear Malcolm, don't you know that decisions about hiring are made a year in advance. If you wanted to be hired, you should have said so before you went abroad.   That is the trivial reason.

I considered waiting out another year, or asking the mathematics department for a job (my skills were good but my course credits were less impressive—had I gone there I should probably have wound up at Los Alamos or at Bletchley). I wound up instead at Law School. As it turned out, not a bad choice. Having lunch with Mortimer Adler, I mentioned my turn-down by the Philosophy Department. He said 'We need you at the Law School'. (Mortimer, although not a lawyer and not a member of the Law School Faculty, had made himself, characteristically, a power in the Law School.) Having just learned my lesson, I said, Well, the decisions about Law School Admissions have already been completed. He said, That's all right. I'll tell the Dean to admit you. He did. The Dean did. So I became a lawyer.

The deeper reason is this—When I come to look back, most of the energies of most professional philosophers is devoted to questions created by philosophers and having little or no value except for professional advancement. That is not, I believe, how it should be. It is not how it was in Socrates' day or Aristotle's. It is a deformation that has grown. A philosophy teacher, I believe, should be someone who has met real problems and then thought about them more deeply. I want philosophy of law to come from lawyers, philosophy of art from artists, philosophy of science from scientists. Philosophy from those who have encountered little more than philosophy seems to me worth very little.

John Dewey, The Need for a Recovery of Philosophy (1917), "Philosophy recovers itself when it ceases to be a device for dealing with the problems of philosophers and becomes a method, cultivated by philosophers, for dealing with the problems of men".[59]

I have no recollection of ever having read this, and probably I never did until now, but I agree with it, and it expresses my point of view. Most philosophical writing is directed to empty issues manufactured by philosophy professors. I want philosophers to be physicians, lawyers, businessmen, governors, soldiers, thieves, and to address the problems of their professions with philosophical insight. Go get a job. Be a success at it, or a failure. Then philosophize.

In this spirit, I am writing a book called Philosopher in a Flivver, which seeks to identify and examine philosophical problems that come to mind in connection with driving an automobile, which most of us have had real experience with. If I were now to teach philosophy, I would try to put to use the experience we have as drivers, the experience I have had as a lawyer, my efforts to write music, to paint pictures, to write poetry, my experience as a local politician and as a government official, my experience in business management, as a husband and as a father. If I have thought imaginatively and deeply enough I should have something to offer a philosophy class. Had I been allowed to teach before I had faced these challenges, I should have offered, I fear, mostly empty words.

Empty Words

I am looking at the New York Review, November 16, 1995, reading about Balanchine and Kirstein. My eyes fall on an advertisement for a book, Postmodern Apocalypse, Theory and cultural practice at the end, Richard Dellamora ed., 1995. I have not read the book. It may be a fine book. But this (in its relevant entirety) is what the University of Pennsylvania Press offers in an effort to sell the book.

> "This book examines apocalypse in contemporary cultural practice and explores the ways in which the post-apocalyptic in contemporary cultural practice becomes post-modern in the works of late twentieth-century writers, filmmakers, and critics."

Law

Why did I not teach law. Again there is a mixture of trivial and deeper reasons.

After I left law school, I had a job in Washington and then came back to Columbia as a faculty assistant, working for Jules Goebel's Foundation in Legal History, but also assisting Professor Llewellyn and teaching a course with him in Legal Argument. I discussed with Assistant Dean James Gifford the possibility of teaching. He said, sensibly (whether it was intended to put me off gently, I don't know), 'We prefer to hire either people just out of law school or people with many years of experience.' I thought that made sense, especially the preference for many years of real law experience. I can see a course in Contract Law conducted by a young instructor with sharp and fresh insights or a course in Sales Law conducted only by a lawyer of many years of commercial experience. Karl Llewellyn used to say it was best to learn from someone teaching a course for the first time or someone who has been teaching it for twenty years. (But of course he assumed the years of commercial experience behind that).

I went on to become Litigation Supervisor for the National Labor Relations Board, General Counsel of the Office of Alien Property, and a practitioner in New York with a varied but not lucrative practice including international and corporate matters. I then returned to Washington in the Office of Economic Opportunity in charge of Grant matters and litigation, to the Department of Health, Education, and Welfare, in charge of matters that fell between the cracks: Medicaid and Medicare inconsistencies, long-term care, environmental matters; Indian programs; advice to the Office of Grant Policy, later, Chairman of the Departmental Grant Appeals Board.

While in private practice, I lost a case I thought I should not lose[60], and questioned whether I was qualified to teach law if I could be so flatly wrong in predicting the outcome of a case.

Certainly, I was qualified to teach Alien Property Law, but while there was money to be made by lawyers in that field (I did not make it), it was a self-limiting field—there was no reasonable need for a law school course in the subject. I did conduct for Professor Walter Gellhorn a session of an administrative law seminar on that subject. He later reciprocated by addressing a session of my course in Grant Practice at the University of South Carolina.

And certainly, I was qualified to teach grant law. I created a syllabus on the subject and found no interest in the law schools. Harvard said I was too old. I offered to correct that, but they didn't buy. The Washington area law schools clearly should have wanted it, because of the large slice of the federal budget involved, because of the unusual legal problems presented, and because of the way in which it cut across several other fields, constitutional law, statutory drafting, administrative law, and others. Only the University of South Carolina invited me to teach it, which I did by arrangement with HEW, and they asked me to come permanently. My wife Irma, however, was rightly unwilling to move away from her excellent doctor, Harold Silver, so I did not go.

I have consistently worked my way into the unrewarding and unteachable corners of the fields I have worked in. This represents some happenstance, but also, I believe, a personality trait.

I am not an expert in international banking, which would be financially rewarding and also a teachable subject. I was an expert in the World War II treatment of international banking, which could be financially rewarding if you have your eye out for the main chance (I didn't) and is hardly a subject for a teaching career.

I am not an expert in Government contract law, which would be financially rewarding and which the law schools enthusiastically teach. I am an expert in government grant law. The Bar Associations tuck us in with contract law where we don't belong. The Universities cannot be convinced that we are a separate subject from government contract law, have separate problems, more interesting problems, and involve government spending in roughly as great or much greater amounts.

I am not an expert in Bankruptcy Law. I have some expertise in Chapter X Bankruptcy, a branch of the law now repealed. (Of course, if I were sufficiently motivated, I could acquire expertise in Chapter XI and other chapters of the Bankruptcy laws, but I am not).

I am not sure what this spells out, but I know it is typical of my history. Had I been a little shallower here and a little wider there I should have done better.

4/2/95

History

Someone, I don't remember who, said Jews worship a God-in-History. I am not sure I understand what he meant, or that his pronouncement means much. Many peoples have believed that their ups and downs reflect God's rewards and punishments for their faithfulness, or lack, to His rules. Many peoples have preserved their lists of kings and pedigrees. Perhaps few have preserved as rich a history over so long a period. (Chinese? Indians?).

I felt very much at home searching XIIth and later XVth century records for Jules Goebel and inventing methods of interpretation. My language gifts helped me find meaning, read handwritings.

I am deeply committed to history. Why do I write family history, personal history. Why do I date my notes so that their sequence could be reestablished. Why do I preserve personal archives, correspondence, chron files, in obvious excess. Family history has of course become fashionable and I have become historian in part by seniority in our branch of a large family but in part because I have a special interest in preserving memory of our characters and quirks and insights and mysteries that others (except perhaps Jimmy M., my young first cousin once removed) do not have as intensely.

Jewish-learning, the Talmud, is history carrying ideas. (Why do we preserve in our commentaries that Rabbi Antigones taught . . . rather than just preserve what he taught?). Whatever I learn I tend to look to origins: etymology, mathematics, law. [And yet, less than most of the Friday group have I read strongly recommended biography].

2/25/95

Lectures

The ghetto of say 1900 had a great appetite for lectures on any subject at all. You didn't have to learn, you just wanted the bells of knowledge to ring in your ears. Free lecture on astronomy, socialism, literature,[61] anything intellectual is good. Perhaps the lack of intensive concentration on the Talmud left a vacuum, but Talmud study had been primarily for men while the ghetto lectures invited women equally.

4/16/95

Today, almost a century after the ghetto lectures, there is a great spurt [not only among Jews] of Book Clubs, Great Books discussion, and Elderhostels and Institutes for Learning in Retirement.

5/15/96

Gabe used to spend summers at a resort in Maine. While there, he offered to give weekly lectures on literature and philosophy, which became very popular.

My mother-in-law, Anne Kates, decided to go to a resort for the summer. She heard of this place and went there but did not know that my uncle went there. When she came in, the receptionist said, Oh, I'm sorry, I'm afraid you have come too late for the lecture.—What lecture?—Why, don't you know, Dr. Mason's weekly lecture. Many people come for that.

As I have already noted, by Hofstadter's count, I probably am e-lingual—that is I speak about 2 ¾ languages—perhaps more (English, French and bits of others).

Dictionaries

I have French-French dictionaries, 4 or more,
    German-German several
    Italian-Italian
    Spanish-Spanish

I have two thesauruses in French (Dictionnaire des Idées Sugérées par les Mots; Dictionnaire analogique); and one in Yiddish.

When I cannot get or work with a same-language dictionary, I prefer to go through some other language. I am not sure that has a real value. It may be foolish, but I steer away from X-English.

    Portuguese-German
    Italian-French
    German-French
    Hebrew-Aramaic-Arabic-German
    Hebrew-French

The advantage I believe I have in using by preference a same-language dictionary is first, that I believe that I get a truer sense of the real meaning of a word and its usage; second, that I learn a lot more by chasing down the meaning of a word and its defining words, and usages; third, the advantage of peripheral noting of other words in the same part of the alphabet; fourth, that I am forced to try to think in the language when I try to guess a word to use and look it up.

I also have, however, Russian-English
Norwegian-English
And also French-English (inherited from CGG) and an excellent French-English, gift of SHSL

> Spanish-English
> Latin-English and Latin grammar
> German-English
> Greek-English (2)
> 26-language dictionary
> Chinese-English (limited)
> Turkish-English and an excellent Turkish grammar
> Several travelers handbooks, Modern Greek, Romanian, Multi-language

Also Yiddish-English and Yiddish-Hebrew-English and a Yiddish grammar

Hebrew-English (2) and several Hebrew grammars
Others

And some vocabularies that belong to record sets: Russian, Hebrew, Chinese, Japanese. Also some Army Manuals in Japanese, Chinese (Mandarin and Cantonese) and a State Department manual in Hebrew.

I have also done some reading—little—in
    Provençal
    Gaelic (medical)
    Romanian (legal)
    Chinese—first without and then with the records
    Japanese—first without and then with the records
    Sanskrit
    Dutch
    Norwegian
    Danish
    Samoan
    Hawaiian
    Ladino

The Adirondacks have French-Canadian families—for example Gokie—originally Gauthier. When a major hurricane swept through, French-Canadian lumberjacks came down to clear the woods. I learned some of their vocabulary. I have read novels in French-Canadian (Marie Blaise).

When Irma and I visited Arizona and several Native American tribes there, I was offered a lesson in Pima. The method was a series of slides with voice-over describing the scene. After a while, I confessed that I could not hear the difference between the word for blue and the word for green. My instructor jumped up and down and chortled, You've got it! You've got it! (Pima, like several other languages, does not distinguish between blue and green.)

Labor complaint

At the Brussels Inter-Allied Reparations Agency meeting that I attended, there were two official languages, English and French. There were accordingly two teams of interpreters. The standard rule of interpreters is that you translate from a language you know well into your mother tongue, not the other way. It was a game to use obscure idioms to see what the interpreters would make of it. For example, the British would say, What you gain on the swings, you lose on the roundabouts, an idiom from county fairs, and laugh when the English to French translators thought it referred to the length of a highway.

I chose to speak in French, partly no doubt to show off, but also because it forced people to listen and partly to disprove the prejudice that Americans cannot speak other languages. Most of the delegates could speak English or French equally well. One day, the conference director took me aside. Because I spoke French, most of the delegates had also chosen to speak French. The French to English team had complained that they had had to do most of the work while the English to French team had it easy. He asked me to speak English. I said, Sorry, but the rules of the conference provide that each delegate could speak in his choice of either of the two official languages.

1/5/03

Counting

Don Adolfo Kates, my mother-in-law's second husband came to Cuba from Belgium. He spoke an excellent Spanish, but when he did arithmetic, he always thought in Vlämsh.

When I do exercises, I count in Turkish. In other contexts, I count in Mandarin or in Hebrew. This is not a recurring to an early tongue like Don Adolfo's Vlämsh, but I do not think I consciously decide what language to use. Hebrew seems to come in the kitchen, when I am cooking. I think Mattie, my housekeeper for some 30 years, used to believe I was saying a prayer when I counted out loud achat, shtaim, shalosh, arba . . . .

Don Adolfo's son José took us somewhere by car. When he parked the car, a kid came over and asked. Watch your car, mister?

I think the implication was, if you paid them to "watch your car" nothing bad would happen to it. Otherwise, they might see to it that it did. José said, No me molesta, chico, and walked away. Having established that he was not a tourist, he was confident that his car was safe.

Latin languages (others, no doubt, also) seem to have a taste for learned and elegant discussion of the fine points—the exact differences of similar expressions. In Havana, I read two such books in Spanish that probably belonged to José. I have also read similar columns in a Spanish newspaper, in a French newspaper, in an Italian newspaper, and some in a Yiddish newspaper.

1/10/03

Don Adolfo and a group of friends also had a historic Spanish (and before that an Indian) mud bath surrounded by a group of houses. One time we visited it, took the mud bath and stayed over night. About 4 A.M. the charcoal burners came down from the mountains on a path, heading for town. They talked in loud voices, but we did not understand what they said. Was it Basque?

I left Irma and the kids and the maid in Havana, while I went to Brussels. They stayed at Don Aldolfo's finca, a farm in the country with a farmer and a big dog, Marquesa. I believe the first words our son Mike uttered were Fuera, Marquesa, get out of here, Marquesa.

When we got back to the States, we had an apartment in New York but I worked in Washington, living in the Y (18th and G Street) and came home every Friday. Irma would hand me Jan (with the colic) and recuperate. Whenever I took Mike to Riverside Drive, I murmured to him a poem by Ronsard (Comme on void sur la branche au mois de may la rose) (original spelling) and I identified for him (in English) everything we passed—

sycamore ball (baw), airplane (air bay). When I took Jan, I murmured another Ronsard (Mignonne, allons voir si la rose). I felt they would benefit from having it in their ear.

When Mike was born, my mother asked, Does he have good feet? We said yes.—Then he will be able to stand on them. (She was right.) Surprisingly early, he was able to turn himself over and to hold his head up. When we tried to get him to skip his 2 A.M. feeding, we couldn't. But soon, when he was ready, he slept through the night. Our friend, Sarah Lowenthal, wife of Abe Lowenthal, our friend and later my law partner, called Mike and Jan at 4 and 3, Hopalong and Shlepalong. We cherished the closing picture of the Family of Man showing a brother and sister of about those ages, walking away in a style that earns Sarah's characterization. It is not a picture of Mike and Jan, but you could swear it is. Mike (about 5) loved the musical, Oklahoma! (Homa) and he listened to the record over and over. We were pleased with his taste but we feared that he didn't understand that a phonograph was a delicate machine. We asked him, if you had a little boy who played the phonograph and didn't understand that it was breakable, how would you stop him. Mike answered, you can't stop him. He has to stop hisself. Mike was a leader in mischief and in achievement. He was an organizer, an actor, a property man, captain of a soccer team, a blue ribbon rider. Very early, he startled his teacher by discovering and reporting that the sum of successive odd numbers gives you the successive square numbers ($1+3+5+7=4^2$; $1+3+5+7+9=5^2$; and so on). We took Mike to be tested at the NYU Psychology Laboratory. He failed to make the 99th percentile because the student who tested him (I assume it was a student) asked him how much is 3 x 7. Mike, pre-kindergarten, answered, Don't ask me how much is 3 x 7. Ask me how much is 33 x 37 and I'll tell you. (He would have.) The foolish student put him down as not able to answer the 3 x 7 question. A few years later, Mike was going to Steiner School, where from the earliest grades, students learn

German and French in addition to English. We had a German businessman for dinner. Hearing that Mike spoke German, he asked in German how much is 43 x 49. Mike answered correctly in German and it was obvious he was not translating but thinking in German.   He published at school an unauthorized newspaper and insisted on his First Amendment right to do so. He attended the trial of the Black Power leaders and wrote an account of it that was published in an alternative newspaper (Irma and I thought it a very good job).   After high school, he organized an outing group, hired a bus and driver to transport the group, coped with occasional mishaps.   He studied a college age TV question show, and, although he was tense, passed himself off as the kind of laid-back kid he saw they were looking for, was taken on, and surprised us one day by telling us to watch the TV program: he was going to be on it. (He did well, won some money but not the grand prize.)   He organized a baseball team that played in the Central Park league.   Jan, who believes in the rebirth of souls, says that in a previous life, Mike was a general.

I have the Encyclopaedia Britannica XIth edition and also the 1959 edition. My daughter, son-in-law and granddaughters have the Columbia Cyclopedia, the Junior Britannica and Mortimer Adler's edition.   One day my granddaughter Sharan phoned me. She had to write a paper on Borromean rings. Knowing that my answer would be, Look it up, she forestalled me by saying, I tried to look it up in the Encyclopaedia, Grampy, but I can't find it. So I told her, this refers to a set of three rings no two of which interlock but the set of three do. (Such a set used to be the logo for a brand of beer—I think Pabst Blue Ribbon . . .) I still don't know who assigned it, or why it was considered an appropriate assignment for a middle school student.

12/11/96

In many languages contradictory meanings overlap:

> We have let = prevent and let = allow;
> trip = walk nimbly and trip = stumble;
> oversight = careful management and oversight = careless error
> pitted = having pits and pitted = having the pits removed;
> shelled = having shells and shelled = having the shells removed;
> ravel = entangle and ravel = disentangle;
> sanction = approval and sanction = enforcement of disapproval;
> cleave = adhere and cleave = separate;
> but also, less obvious, black, bleak, bleach, blank, blanch are siblings;
> blessed = bloody;
> in some languages strong and weak are the same (I think in Egyptian).

See also earlier discussion of law principles verbally inconsistent (Chapter Learning, p. 181) and passage on dreams, Irma and Leonardo Da Vinci (Starting, p. 97).

11/22/02

Speaking in tongues

I take pleasure, often, in declaiming meaningless word sounds. These are sometimes light, sometimes heavier, most often Slavic sounds although not really Slavic words. An example invented to illustrate:

Shlóvo perúshnaya atzér ikáye bo. Avladánya yastronájik pushkárdzik krashádzik avruátye.

3/29/03

Suffixes

I spend a lot of time, often instead of sleeping, listing words with a particular ending, trying to see which are definitely suffixes (which are happenstance), what is their meaning, what they add to the root, how they modify the root, which work on adjectives, which on verbs, which on nouns, which work not on English roots, which occurred before English developed. Here is a sampling that kept me awake for an hour last night (12-1):—th

bath, both (ambo?), birth, berth (bear), mirth (merry), girth (gird), breadth (broad), length (long), width (wide), depth (deep), but not heighth, tallth.

broth (brew), froth, firth, forth, booth, growth, kith, pith, worth, cloth, dearth (dear), earth [er], hearth, heath, month (moon), south (sun), north, but not easth,westh.

doth, hath, fourth, fifth etc, filth, truth (true), ruth (rue), sooth, tooth, mouth (maw), wealth (weal), health (heal, hale), stealth (steal), wraith, wrath, wroth, breath, myth, path, plinth, swath, uncouth, youth (young) but not oldth.

When Mike was a young preteen, he invented the word pauce from the analogy scarce: scarcity::?: paucity, I told him that language was not always so logical. (But I was delighted.)

2/1/95

When I was about ten or so, I went to the Talmud Torah of the YMHA that was about 2 or 3 long blocks from where we lived on Boston Road. The principal was Simon Rifkind, later a Judge of the N.Y. Supreme Court (trial court) and then after resigning from the court a practicing lawyer. When his firm (notably a partner, Morris Abram), represented our hospitals in litigations, I dropped in to tell Judge Rifkind I was one of his graduates.⁶² When the Talmud Torah elected a "student government" or "general organization", Judge, then Mr. Rifkind presided. I said he should not preside: we should choose a student chairman "pro tem". He asked whether I knew what pro tem meant. Of course, I did. (Probably) thereupon this knowledge made me chairman pro tem. I then ran for some student office and with my father's advice I made and put up posters showing my name on a square box: "Vote for Mason. He's on the square." This had meaning to him but what meaning did it have for me or the preteen electorate? I remember the posters. I don't remember whether I was elected. Probably yes. Only much later did I return to elective politics.

In Talmud Torah I learned enough Hebrew to extemporize in Hebrew an extended narrative. With a coach (melamed) I practiced my bar mitzvah passages and had enough Hebrew to write my own Hebrew speech (thanking my parents and commenting on my passage from the prophets (Micah 4:1-4), rejecting the canned speech my melamed offered me—although my uncle Gabe had accepted a canned speech. Yet no one explained to me the meaning of the non-vowel points that floated under and over the Hebrew letters. When I asked, I was given a brush-off answer, that said they were unimportant, had a meaning but one I did not have to know. Only many years later did I learn (from Professor Binder's book on cantillation) that they were a superbly delicate system of punctuation and at the same time a notation of the music to which the words were to be chanted. They are traditionally regarded as essential to a correct understanding of the biblical text. An orthodox boy learns the cantillation as a matter of course. Oscar Gass, shown my Hutter Bible, put on a hat and chanted (I assume correctly. It sounded right).

Later, I learned Israeli Hebrew from State Department tapes and texts, which I paid for. Again I became temporarily fluent. [The OEO certified that I needed the training because on my trip to Israel

I would inquire into community organization, which I did at no great depth—The Department did not require a deep need and there was no government cost except perhaps a recordkeeping one].

I picked up a smattering of Jewish music and cantillation from Dr. Binder who lectured at Cooper Union on a survey of Jewish music. Years later I met him again as head of the music department at Stephen Wise Free Synagogue.

He taught a few of us to chant the brochas (blessings), disregarding as was proper the fact that I was a non-singer. When I said that I missed from our services the beautiful setting we sang in the Jackson Avenue Synagogue, of the Ki Mitzion [for out of Zion goes forth the Law, which comes from my bar mitzvah haftarah passage], he scornfully told me that was not Jewish music but German music, which it was, as shown by the use of scale and sequences. Still I loved it and missed it. He taught me to chant, among others, the brocha for wine, but I later disgraced myself in the Synagogue of Aix en Provence [where I had gone looking for Milhaud's Synagogue] when told to drink a cup of wine that the rabbi had passed to me hand to hand after he and the hazan had blessed it, (presumably recognizing me as an American and assuming perhaps I was a rich American) I was startled into drinking it without the brocha which I could have chanted convincingly in the Ashkenazi style (although this was a Sephardic service). [My warm reception up until then became conspicuously cold—I assume for that reason.]

3/7/95

We were slaves

Every year, in the special service for the Passover celebrated at home in even barely Jewish families, we are reminded that we were slaves in Egypt. Not just our ancestors, but we ourselves. This service is for what God did for *me* when he took me out of Egypt.

It is also Jewish tradition that when the Ten Commandments were handed down at Mount Sinai, we ourselves were there, not just our ancestors but we ourselves, and said to each commandment, 'We will do so and we will hear'. Although, 'we will hear' means we will obey, there lingers a special flavor in the fact that we agree to do before we agreed to hear.

I do not know any Jew who believes simply we, we ourselves, were slaves in Egypt, but we are reminded at least annually of our reasons for empathy with the poor, the oppressed, the slaves, of all centuries, and in America, the Blacks. And we are impressed with the idea that the basic morality of Mount Sinai was voluntarily accepted by us. A Jewish folktale says that the Ten Commandments were first offered to each of the various peoples of the world and that only the Jews said, Yes, we'll take it.

A story about the vitz (joker), Motke Chabad, says that when the Ten Commandments were being handed down, Motke went along until they came to Lo Sinof, Thou shalt not commit adultery. That, he would not accept. Pointing out that Moses himself was not pure in that respect (as noted earlier, the Bible is not clear on this point, but folk tradition is: 'the Cushite woman that he took' Numbers 12.1, 'Asher lakach'[63]), Motke threatened to get the rest of the Jews not to accept this commandment. God and Moses were forced to make a deal with him—that he should have a private exception. Then, with the exception, he accepted it and let the crowd accept it.

This teaching, that we were slaves in Egypt (and oppressed in Persia, and down through the ages) has made Jews throughout history, more than most recognizable ethnic groups, 'liberal', and 'radical', and, in XXth Century America, more than most inclined to be Democrats and to be sympathetic to Black aspirations. Not exclusively so, but more than randomly so.

A complication: In the South, it was the Republicans, the party of Lincoln, that first claimed the allegiance of Blacks and of those sympathetic to their needs. But over the years, there was a game of Puss-in-the-corner, Democrats became Republicans, and it was the party of Jesse Helms, Pat Buchanan, Strom Thurmond, Newt Gingrich, Bob Dole, Trent Lott, that failed the Blacks.

Another complication: In New York City, a decent person had to be a Democrat in national politics, to be sure, but could be a Republican in local politics, because local politics was dominated by Tammany Hall. Which you would become, if you made a political commitment, might depend on the timing of your commitment or on whether your interests in politics were more local or more national. The Sylvester and Medaglie families, active in City politics, were Republicans. Hubert Humphrey and Mrs. Roosevelt came into New York City and supported Tammany candidates.

1932 was a watershed year. My mother's family and, I presume, my mother, had been Republican in the 1920s. In the 1930s, she, and all close to us were 'of course' Roosevelt Democrats. Our cousin Charles Rits announced, however, that he was a Republican and would vote against Roosevelt. I remember the shock with which this was received by our family, who thought it impossible that a Jew should vote Republican.

My uncle Gabe was a self-described rebel, but an American patriot. To me, as a child, that was a strange confrontation. Gabe was a Socialist Party official at a time when New York State considered socialism an offense[64], and later a Liberal Party official. My father was a socialist but without formal affiliation so far as I know. As a child of 7, I distributed Socialist Party flyers for the election campaign of Morris Hillquit, running for Mayor of New York. He was not elected.

7/30/96

Anarchy

We Jews have a built-in tendency toward anarchy. That does not exclude the fact that we also have a countervailing tendency toward organization. We make sects, we make splits, we reject heretics.

But the Bible tells us, In those days, there was no king in Israel. Each man did that which appeared right in his own eyes. (Judges 21.25).

The Bible tells us that when the people clamored for a king, they were told they would regret it. (1. Sam. 8, 11-18).

Judaism has no central authority, no Pope. The authority of every commentator must stand on the persuasiveness of his arguments and his reputation for learning and wisdom.

My great uncle Anshel and his wife Miriam (Wiersbolowsky) left Russia for Vienna where they lived under an assumed name (Markel) and she wrote under that assumed name. I do not know but guess that this was in the period 1860-1881 when there were anarchist plots, ultimately successful, to assassinate Tsar Alexander II. The Jewish Encyclopedia refers to their expatriation discretely as a time of family troubles but I assume that they (or he) were implicated, or merely suspected of participation in the plots or of having knowledge of the plotters. Years later (by 1895) they had resumed the family name and it appeared on her books (published by cousins in Warsaw, the Brothers Levin-Epstein) so they must have felt the danger had passed. The Levin-Epstein family was later active in developing the Dental School in Palestine. My uncle Herman and my brother visited them in 1935.

My seemingly bourgeois uncle Herman (that is, he was relatively wealthy, with a strong interest in good food, in books, in the arts, a photographer, a movie maker, an opera goer, a play goer, a business man) was a friend of the anarchists Emma Goldman and Alexander Berkman[65]. My uncles Herman and Gabe with, I must assume, the concurrence of their brothers, sheltered the anarchist editor Claus Timmermann, who was, it was rumored, from 1916 or 1917 on, sought by the police [perhaps in connection with the plot to assassinate the steel magnate, Henry Clay Frick or perhaps just for opposition to the draft?]. The family were friends of the anarchist painter and sculptor Modest Stein and his wife Marcia, an excellent photographer in the then advanced artistic portrait school. I have a belief, based on almost nothing, that Herman remained a bachelor because he had hoped to marry Marcia. Modest was also a friend of Claus Timmermann and was clearly involved in the Frick plot. At Claus's funeral, eulogies were offered by Modest and my uncle Gabe. (Some of this is touched on by Professor Avrich in a history of Anarchists in America and in his Anarchist Voices).[66] Claus was given undemanding jobs at camp in the Berkshires. One year, as the family left camp, Herman asked Claus, Do you know how to hang wall paper? Oh, yah. Well, here's the wall paper and the paste. Some time in the Winter, put this paper up in the living room of the house on the hill.   When the family came back in the Spring, Herman said, I see you got the wall paper up, but what are those bumps. Claus looked and exclaimed, Jaysus Christ, I for-got to take the pic-tures down. He used his own name, so the notion that he was in hiding cannot have been very real.   The Stein's daughter Luba was a teenage friend of my sister (Bryna). Their son (so I recently thought, but more likely a neighbor's son) was a sculptor in an Art Deco style. They lived, at one time, across Forest Avenue from my grandparents.

When I argued in my quarterly newsletter that Administrative Law Judges could and should consider the constitutionality of the laws they had to apply (they are generally instructed to assume the validity of laws and regulations), Walter Gellhorn sagely wrote me that that could lead to anarchy. I replied both to him and publicly that I understood that; anarchy was part of my tradition.[67] Walter was taken aback and remarked that I would not have ventured to say that in the time of

McCarthy. Perhaps not, but I have tried to do that which appeared right in my own eyes. When some of McCarthy's Senate Committee successors ordered me repeatedly and insistently to turn over to their committee, documents that, if leaked, could have been a death warrant for an innocent man, as they knew, I did not do so. They complained to President Nixon. Egil Krogh summoned me to the White House and ordered me "and I speak for the President on this" to comply. I still did not do so. I delivered, as I had offered from the beginning, expurgated copies, labeled as such. They did leak, as I expected, the expurgated documents I gave them. If the pressures had been greater, I might have complied. I don't know. But I think my non-compliance was right.

4/18/98

Agenda

It is part of my personal religion, one that I find many people share instinctively, that a job-to-be-done has more rights than people's status. If someone is carrying a heavy or awkward package, you hold the door, or wait, or step aside. There is, of course, an opposing principle that some people act on ('I am the important one. You step aside for me'. What strain of people act on that principle?)   but most of us respect the precedence of the task—the task itself—anybody's task.

Greek agein, to drive, to lead, to carry, Latin agere also, mean to observe as a religious rite.

1/22/96

Schadenfreude and Envy

I have a bad character and it gets worse with age. I have to admit to myself that when I see a photograph or a cartoon of

Yasser Arafat I feel a twinge of pleasure in noting that his face and especially his mouth is ugly. It is momentary, and passes quickly and I reject the idea at once that I am entitled to hate him because he is ugly or to draw an inference of moral ugliness from his physical ugliness. But I am forced to recognize that this flash of nastiness in my mind is not very different in kind from the pleasure many Germans took in cartoons of ugly Jews in Der Stuermer, even if it differs in quantity and in acceptance.

Similarly, I acknowledge a moment of pleasure when I see Gingrich caught behaving badly. I believe he is a bad person and harmful to our country but exposure of his personal misbehavior should not give me pleasure even if it makes an effective argument against some of his claims.

I also recognize that when I read of someone getting some preferment, I am not free of thoughts that I could have done that job or had that preferment and perhaps should have.

In Kennedy's time, I think, (perhaps Johnson's), I was recommended for a federal Judgeship. I did not get it. The recommendation was political although based on a reasonable judgment of merit. My rejection may have been political but may have been on the merits. I know that at least one well-informed person consulted by the Attorney General (Bobby Kennedy? Katzenbach?) advised that I had limited trial experience, which was true, although some excellent judges have had no more than I. I am not troubled by the fact that I did not get it, but when I read that X or Y did get it, I admit that I sometimes feel a passing whiff of envy.

These are not good. I am glad that they pass quickly. I think that with age they occur more often than they did when I was younger. I believe that age allows some bad traits to surface more readily, like the use of swear words.

1/12/95

Floating

I float: My attention always moves to the higher theoretical issues. In fields in which I am truly expert (alien property, grants) I am always conscious of how ignorant I am of details that are of "merely practical" importance. Others, who have much less grasp than I of fundamental theoretical issues, often know what they have to know to be effective practitioners, things that I don't know and am not very interested to learn. I know the OMB Circulars are not sound. They know that the latest amendment of OMB Circular A-110 has the following practical problems . . . Foreigners with alien property problems knew where the shoe pinched them. On specifics they often knew the intricacies of rules where I knew only the purpose and general effect. Broker-dealer clients knew SEC rules in the detail that affected them. I had a fairly good understanding of the purpose and approach. Karl Llewellyn used to say . . . ' Some parts of law practice require ready answers . . . But the fish stink and demurrage is piling up . . . '[68] Rules of evidence are only semi-rational. The rational part, I had a good knowledge of. The non-rational part, I more or less knew but never had the tip of the tongue practical working knowledge of. Somehow, I bluffed through, but it was always a matter of great tension. In this, I was handicapped by the Adler-Michael distortion, which sought to emphasize the rational and hide the irrational elements.

1997

Shrimp

In my school years, I was younger than my classmates, shorter, slighter, less sophisticated. I thought of myself as a shrimp. That view of myself I have carried into my age when it is not or should not be true. On reflection I can see that, but my instinctive assumption is normally that others are older, wiser, bigger, stronger, better informed than I.

As a young boy, I skipped four consecutive terms at school under a system intended to keep bright children challenged and interested. This had, unfortunately, the effect that I was in classes with children older, bigger, and socially more sophisticated than I. It also meant that I never had the classes in which I would have learned how to deal with fractions. Since I was naturally fairly gifted in math, I soon caught up on the principle. But I had missed the drill and my knowledge stayed theoretical rather than practical and ingrained. Perhaps something similar was true of sex.

When I was 20, I was tall and thin, as my father had been at that age as shown in photographs. I was a sliver under 5 ft. 11. He was then, at 50, only 5 ft. 8. At the time, I thought this reflected a widely accepted phenomenon—that children of immigrants tended to be bigger and stronger than their parents. I did not then know that he had undoubtedly shrunk as I also did later. By say age 70, I too was only 5 ft. 8 and now at 87, to my amazement, only 5 ft. 6.

In college, at 5 ft. 11, I weighed 109 lbs. and was too heavy to wrestle in the 108 lb. class (105 plus 3 lbs. leeway), so I wrestled in the 118 lb. class, out-classed by 6 to 9 lbs. Once, on the instruction of my coach, I "made the weight" by using the steam room, but that was a bad idea. In my sophomore year, I weighed 119 lbs. and had to wrestle in the 128 lb. class. As a junior, I weighed 129 lbs. and had to wrestle in the 138 lb. class. In my senior year, I weighed 139 lbs. and had to wrestle in the 148 lb. class. 67 years later, I weigh about 179.

11/23/95

A Profile
Notes about myself

1. I like young children and am fairly good in dealing with them.

2. I have a great deal of patience.

3. I have a strong ability to put things into context.

4. I lack empathy.

5. I lack outgoing enthusiasm. The lack of these qualities makes me a less than great teacher.

6. Karl Llewellyn, who was a great teacher, thought me a great teacher, however, and a few of the people who have worked for me—including some who became my friends and some who did not—are very aware of having learned a great deal from me.

7. I have little interest in sports, none in sport news. I have some skills particularly in single sports rather than team sports. I was by skill, not by strength, a good wrestler, a good fencer, but not a good baseball player.

8. I have a strong language sense, an ability to learn languages easily with a feeling for the qualities of different languages. I am weakest in formal grammar and strongest in a feeling for style. (My friend Jack Karro had a similar love for languages, but always knew, given a verb, that this was, for example, the second aorist of an i-stem verb; I never did).

9. I write well. People who have no interest in the subjects I write about nevertheless read and enjoy my published writing.

10. I have some understanding of government but little interest in politics or personalities.

11. I have a strong memory.

12. I am intellectually gifted. I don't know my IQ but it is certainly high, not extremely high. I am interested in puzzles and do well in them. I am addicted to crossword puzzles and double crostics, but have not learned how to do British, French, or Italian puzzles well, and find the NY Times puzzles doable but difficult.

13. I have a lot of mathematical ability. At the age of 20 and 30, I was very active in high school and college math, and in symbolic logic, then a little known field. About 60 I published a paper on symbolic analysis of law (drafted long before) that I believe was creative. It was published under an anonymous peer review system, and got some friendly and corrective comment from W.V.O. Quine. I never moved beyond early college math to advanced group theory, topology, tensor analysis, the mathematics needed for work in relativity and quantum physics, for example. But I enjoy reading that kind of mathematics even though I don't understand it. I read for the music, that is, the pattern of the connections of ideas.

14. I am not a leader or organizer, but in spite of weaknesses in this area, I have created or helped maintain successful organizations.

15. I do not make friends easily, but when I have friends, I usually keep them a long time (for life). College friends, from 1926 on: Irwin Langbein, Jack Karro, Ed Friedlander, Sig Timberg, for example. Adnan Ergeneli (Grenoble, 1930). Professional friends: Russ Packard from 1938 about, Marion, Poulsson, Sejersted from 1947 until they died; Fred Joseph, John Siegmund, from about 1967.

16. As a lawyer, I am strong on intuition as to the facts and the law, very strong on counseling, strong on brief-writing. I lack the people-talents of a jury lawyer and the salesman

skills of a great appellate advocate, and most of the skills of negotiation. The part of negotiation that I am good at is perceiving that people's real goals do not always meet head on, and that sometimes both can be achieved by a slanting approach.

(Thursday, December 7, 1995, we had an annual reunion of the Alien Property staff that has been meeting since 1942, John Wolff, who worked for Karl Llewellyn, and later at Alien Property, and now teaches comparative law at Georgetown University Law School, came over to tell me he learned many things from me and has always been grateful for one thing in particular he learned from me: when there was conflict, I would sit down with both sides and say: There has been a misunderstanding. It always cooled things down and often led to a solution. He says he has often done the same since).

As a lawyer, I am strong on the long look ahead. Also weak on getting paid by clients. That's one reason that I was better off working for the government.

17. As a 20-year-old, I was a strong chess player and enjoyed the beauty of the game more than winning. My ability stopped about that point. At Grenoble, when I was 20, I challenged the Grenoble Chess Club, playing blindfolded simultaneously on three boards against their three best (seeing) players. I had never before played blindfolded. I won one, drew one, and lost one by a flagrant mistake. My opponent offered to let me take the move over, but I said the rule is, joué, c'est joué, a move is a move. Since then I have not kept up. I have stopped playing (except with Sharan and Amber). Three move chess puzzles are usually too difficult for me, two-movers sometimes difficult and getting more so.

18. I am frightened of meeting people, talking on the telephone, confronting danger, but try not to show it, and usually succeed.

19. I have a mild talent in drawing and painting, more in creative insight than in hand skill.

20. I have a mild talent for musical composition and an interest in it, although I am very weak in musician's skills. I do not sing, the fault mostly of a bad education, because I love to sing and do not, I think, have an ugly voice—the NY school system is to blame. I do not have an accurate trained ear (like my nephew Fred's, Joe Hirsch's, John Siegmund's). I do not play an instrument well. (I have played violin, piano, recorder, harmonica, poorly). Yet I consider myself a composer, because I love to compose and spend time at it.

21. I have an excessively complicated mind. When I start to say or write anything, including these notes, I immediately think of complications, exceptions, explanations, qualifications. I try to simplify.

22. My children think I am arrogant and judgmental. Most of my friends who know me otherwise than as their father think otherwise, I believe.

23. I am a generalist with a mental attic filled with a great deal of trivial and non-trivial knowledge of a very wide range and with skill in getting information in many fields.

Well it's after 4AM. Maybe I'll stop here. Wait, a little more.

24. I am self-indulgent and a preserver of excess things and especially paper, and a deliberate preserver of household

disorder. I feel it is essential to my creativity. Irma wanted neatness. She resented but tolerated my disorder.

25. I am also in the process of writing an elaborate autobiography of a sort. It may possibly give a very different picture of my picture of myself.

26. I crave feedback. When I write a letter, I wait anxiously for an answer. When I ask a question, I look for an answer. When someone comments on something I have written, I read it again to try to see how that person saw it.

27. I am very self-critical, always very aware of what I see as defects in me and my work. I don't say I am fully or adequately or accurately aware of all mistakes, but aware of mistakes.

OK, call it a night.

28. I do not like to make advance commitments. Irma knew however, that I would always try to do more than had been indicated. When we married, we did not marry forever—formally, of course, we did, but our private agreement was for 20 years. After 20 years we renewed it for 20 years. After that 20 years, we renewed it for a third 20 years, but we did not reach that mark.

My reluctance to make advance commitments made it difficult for Irma and me to plan vacation travel. I would prefer, when the time came, to just get up and go, but of course it was often necessary to get a passport, make reservations, buy tickets.

The best vacation I ever had was in the 40s, when Pop said I was overworked and must take time off. I went down to the bus station (in NY) and asked where the next bus was going. Atlantic City? Fine. I went to Atlantic City, stayed about a week and went to the Bus

Station. The next bus? Charleston, SC. Fine. I went to Charleston. Stayed a week. Next Bus? St. Petersburg, FL. Fine. I went to St. Petersburg, stayed about a week and went home.

This reluctance to make advance commitment is behind my response when charities ask how much I will pledge, or may we put you down for a pledge. I reply, I never pledge. I may send you a contribution, not a pledge.

1/2/96

29. Curiosity. I have a great deal of curiosity. When I don't know something or don't understand something I run into, I generally ask what? Or why? My friends often chide me for asking questions about things I have no apparent need to know. I don't agree with them. A trivial but typical example: The Book World mentions a book and puts a symbol I had never seen before in front of the title. An arrow pointing to a rectangle that suggests a TV screen. What does it mean? Why do you want to know? Are you thinking of buying the book? No. Are you interested in the author? No. Are you interested in the publisher? No. SO why do you want to know? What use is that information to you? I don't know, but I have never seen that sign before, and I would like to know.

1/5/96

30. 'Fairitude'. [Bryna's word]. I have a strong impulse to see another side to an argument. I despise House Speaker Newt Gingrich and what he is doing. If someone attacks him, I am glad to see him attacked, but if I believe that attack is not fair, I generally will point that out. Example: Gingrich's attack on the book deal of his Democratic predecessor,

Jim Wright, was mean, and it is amusing that Gingrich, as soon as he could, got into a questionable book deal of his own, but let's recognize that Wright's book deal was improper and that Gingrich's book deal was not as improper and not for the same serious reasons. Stop for now.

Moreh Nebuchim

(GUIDE TO THE PERPLEXED)

A young man went to visit his Kaleh (bride-to-be) and her family. The bride's family were noted talmudists. The young man was not. As he left, his rabbi said, surely there will be much talk of talmud, and we know you will not be able to hold your own in that kind of talk. I will give you a hint. Whatever is said, you say the opposite. Perhaps they will think you know more than you do. Sure enough, the talk soon turned to talmud. His mechutan (father-in-law to be) expressed a view. The young man politely interposed the opposite view. One of the elders said, young man, I am afraid you are mistaken. Rashi says the same thing as your mechutan. No, says the young man, Just the opposite. Rashi says the opposite. Another of the elders says, there is no shame in making a mistake. Maimonides, in his Moreh Nebuchim, says the same as your mechutan. No, says the young man, the Moreh Nebuchim says just the opposite. There is no need to quarrel aobut it, says another. The Moreh Nebuchim is there on the shelf. Let us take it down and see. No, says the young man, Just the opposite, let us not take it down.

For those who may wish to take it down, here are notes for this chapter.

[1] *Paul*: Paul G. Dembling was General Counsel of the National Advisory Committee for Aeronautics and of the National Aeronautics and Space Administration and later of the United

States General Accounting Office. He is Senior Counsel of Schnader, Harrison, Segal & Lewis, LLP. He was President of the Federal Bar Association and Chairman of the Section on Public Contract Law of the American Bar Association. He and I have collaborated on several publications in the field of federal grant practice, among them, Dembling and Mason, Essentials of Grant Law Practice (American Law Institute—American Bar Association Committee on Continuing Professional Education, Philadelphia, 1991).

2   *Role of the Lawyer:* Essentials of Grant Law Practice §19.04 (c), p.197

3   *Ito's job*: Ito tried the O.J. Simpson case

4   *Private toilets*: in two offices at 120 Broadway, New York, and one at the HOLC Building, Washington. Of course, I had not asked for them. They were just there before we moved in because the buildings were originally planned for private sector occupancy. Jack Anderson spoke with admiration of Drew Pearson as his employer, mentor and partner. Anderson, in his memoir, Peace, War, and Politics (with Daryl Gibson, Tom Doherty Associates, 1999), 169 says, But when a reporter pulls a whopper, he has an obligation to explain, if he can. His mentor apparently did not follow that code.

5   *Howard Phillips*: Williams v. Phillips, 360 F. Supp. 1363 (1973).

6   *Never get it:* In Current Developments, vol 20, no. 4, p. 16, 'The Uninformed Court', I apply this story to the Justices of the Supreme Court.

7   *Three sets of arms went up*: I remember this happening at 76th and West End Ave., the corner where we lived in the

1950's. Jan, my daughter, remembered it at East 70th Street and 2nd Avenue, near where my sister Bryna lived, and much later. I assume we are both right.

8   V*iziers*: see Silver, The Green Rose, (Dial Press, NY, 1977), La Rosa Verde (Editorial Pomaire, Barcelona, 1979). See ch. I of this book, Starting: 42-44 and note at p. 112.

9   *Hasdai and the princes of the Khazars*: cf. Cecil Roth, A History of the Jews (Schocken Books, NY) 158-159. The kingdom of the Khazars lasted for about 200 years (8th century—10th century) but was invaded (965-969) by the Prince of Kiev. The Princes of the Khazars escaped to Spain where they knew, having corresponded with Hasdai, that they would find influential friends. See first chapter of this book, Starting, Conversion p. 52-55.

10 *Joseph Nasi*: *Naxos*: Roth, 254

11 *Henry of Valois*: Roth, p.255

12 *Prime Minister for a day:* family legend via Gabe via Levinsohn a descendant of Kishiniski.

13 *Unanimous:* Sigismund II (1587-1682) tried unsuccessfully to change this traditional rule, notably in the diet called March 7, 1666.

14 *Nader*: This was written before Nader made a serious campaign for the presidency. Perhaps after 2000, a better example would be, if the Electoral College could not choose between Bush and Gore, they might choose for an overnight role Donna Shalala or Helen Thomas.

15 *Stewards*: Roth 269, 305, 308

17 *The Physician Himself*: There are many editions. I guess the edition I read was 1902. Cathell, A Book About the Physician Himself, F.A. Davis Co., Philadelphia

18 *Coincidences: Witch*: This reference is intended as an allusion to Biblical references to the "book of the kings of Israel" and other books which are not included in the Bible. For example, 2 Chron 25:26: Now the rest of the acts of Amaziah, first and last, behold, are they not written in the book of the kings of Judah and Israel? cf. also 2 Chron 12:15: Now the acts of Rehoboam, first and last, are they not written in the book of Shemaiah the prophet and of Iddo the seer concerning genealogies?

19 *Deficiencies of Adler's approach*: A Theory of Contract Sanctions, 38 Col. L.R.773 (1938) and The Logical Structure of a Proposition of Law. Jurimetrics Journal, March 1971, 99. See chapter II of this book, Learning, Richard Powell, 199-200.   Professor Michael and his wife, Florence, later invited me to dinner so his resentment was not permanent.

20 *Catholic*: I was ignorant of the fact reported in Adler's obituary (Chicago Tribune, July 24, 2001) that he attended an Episcopalian church, not a Catholic church.

21 *Meno*: see Ch. I, Starting, p. 12

22 *Learning is a kind of reminding*: see Randall, Aristoltle (Columbia U. Press 1960) 45.

23 *Books I have meant to write*: it is intended that a section in the last chapter of this book will discuss 'When I consider life and its few years'

24 *General Counsel*: For reasons of office politics, I signed after transfer to the Department of Justice as Chief of the Legal Branch but my Civil Service record read General Counsel.

25. *Let your head save your heels:* See second chapter of this book, Learning, p. 228.

26. *John Schamus*: See second chapter of this book, Learning, p. 196.

27. *Business management*: When we sold GAF, I said in a speech (I think it was for the American Society of International Law) that we expected to sell it for about a hundred million dollars. I was challenged by Dr. Kronstein, who said it was absurd to think we could get even a small part of that. We got much more.

28. *Yiddish I heard as a child*: See note of words and phrases in Yiddish that I heard even though Yiddish was avoided. First chapter of this book, Starting, note, pp. 106-108; see also p. 134, p. 162.

29. *In Paul's time:* There were congregations that were essentially Jewish but accepted Jesus and congregations that were essentially Universalist, in great variety.

30. *Napoleon*: See on this, earlier discussion Chapter Starting, 52-3.

31. *Trickily baptized*: Roth, p. 345-346. Her attack was sustained by the Pope.

32. *Heart is pure*: Cf. Tennyson. Sir Galahad. My Strength is as the strength of ten, Because my heart is pure.

33. *Political Lies*: My cousin Jim Mason is writing a study of John Anderson's race for the Presidency to be published by University Press of America. Anderson made a trip abroad (to Israel, Egypt, Germany, France, England). He met Chancellor Schmidt, Prime Minister Thatcher and officials of Israel, Egypt, and France. This was probably achieved in part, it is said, because Zev Furst visited the Washington

embassies of Britain, France, Germany, and lied to them about having been accepted by the others. Jim intended to tell this story but will drop it because he has one source but could not get it confirmed by a second. See, however, Mark Bisnow, *Diary of a Dark Horse* (Southern Illinois University Press, Carbondale, Ill. 1983, p. 253): "I accompanied Zev to the embassies, and at the time we made our rounds, absolutely no meetings had yet been scheduled for Anderson, nor had even any preliminary approaches been made. This did not prevent Zev, however, from exhibiting his usual self-confident manner. In requesting a meeting with German Chancellor Schmidt, for example, he told German embassy officials that meetings had already been agreed to by Prime Minister Thatcher of Britain and by President Giscard of France. To the British, at a subsequent meeting, he said that Chancellor Schmidt and President Giscard had already agreed. To the French, he said that meetings were already arranged with Chancellor Schmidt and Prime Minister Thatcher. At each embassy, the officials nodded as if impressed, and promised to cable their foreign offices accordingly. The trick seemed to work, because most of the requested appointments with heads of state, foreign ministers, parliamentary officials, and others came through within a couple of weeks."

[34] *Freida Leah visit to Vienna:* It is possible that I have moved the generations down a step. I think I have it right but it is possible that the travellers were Freida Leah and her mother-in-law rather than Freida Leah and her daughter.

[35] *Anarchist plot:* see this chapter, Anarchy, supra

[36] *Reb Itzikl:* cf. Elie Wiesel, Somewhere, a Master, translated from the French by Marion Wiesel, Summit Books NY 1952, pp132-133.

[37] *Psychiatrist—bureaucrat:* J. Gleick, Genius, Panther Books NY, 1992, pp. 223-224

[38] *Babi Yar*: Babi Yar A document in the form of a novel, A. Anatoli Kuznetsov translated by David Floyd, Robert Bentley, Inc., 1970 and the poem Babi Yar by Yevgeni Yevtushenko translated by Benjamin Okopnik, 1996, www.remember.org/witness/babiyar.html

[39] *Karl Llewellyn*: See The Common Law Tradition (Little Brown, 1960), pp. 28, 359-361.

[40] *Correcting distortion*: An exception: a great appellate judge, Harold Leventhal, discussed in my column, Developments in Federal Grant Law, 15 Public Contract Newsletter, no. 3, April 1980, 3.

[41] *New institutions*: cf. my Suit on an Unlicensed Transaction-Singer and the Specie Bank, Pittsburgh L.R., Fall 1954, 16. "The war is over, post-war problems are beginning to yield to a new set of 'Cold-war' problems and we still do not have an intelligible and reliable statement of the most elementary legal question arising under the freezing control, namely, what is the effect of an unlicensed transaction . . . " "When we deal with an institution, such as perhaps testamentary gifts of future interests in real property, which lives in a world that evolves slowly, where even the parties immediately concerned think in long perspectives, there is no disharmony in a judicial process that slowly grinds down a doctrine and takes centuries to arrive at a tolerably clear rule against perpetuities, for example. But we are dealing with an institution created in an emergency to deal with paroxysmal problems, an institution intended for immediate application to a war situation, intended to exhaust its main effects in the period of hostilities, say six years, and the period of immediately post-war settlements, say another four years. When powers so granted in such a statute cannot be elucidated in their most elementary effects for some fifteen years after they were granted, it is evident we are dealing with a judicial process that is not commensurate with the need." p. 30-31.

See also my Current Developments in Federal Grant Law, The Majesty of the Law, 20 Public Contract Newsletter, No. 1, Fall 1984, 6: In Pennhurst v. Halderman (II)[1984] . . . The suit was originally brought in 1974. The undisputed fact findings include a finding that conditions were dangerous, with the residents often physically abused or drugged by staff members. The Court of Appeals held that a remedial order could rest on state law. The Supreme Court, having invited decision on this issue, now held that it could not. It has thus taken 10 years for the courts to contemplate a concededly dangerous condition in an instituition for the mentally retarded . . . There are indeed good reasons why a court should make law slowly and not decide issues that the facts before it do not compel it to decide and the record before it does not justify it in deciding. Yet there is also an important consideration against glacial progress on issues that call urgently for prompt resolution: retarded people being abused, sick elderly people being mistreated. The majesty of justice must proceed with suitable dignity and thoughtfulness, but surely sometimes, in some kinds of cases, it must try to get somewhere in time to do something for someone still living.

[42] *Advocates who do not know the facts*: In the *Stinnes* case, the crux of the case was the effect of an Alien Property order. We had won below on a brief by junior counsel I had approved. Stinnes' Senior Counsel on appeal was a distinguised advocate, but he rejected that brief. Another was written under his instruction. When he was asked by one of the Appellate Division Judges about the order, he simply did not know. He informed the court that Stinnes' president was present and perhaps could explain it. Mr. Rosenthal, Stinnes' president, informed the court that I was present and could perhaps explain it. I gave an impromptu explanation. The outcome was that the court ruled against us but plaintiffs did not enter the decision, knowing that as soon as they did, we would appeal and probably win. So we won by losing.

In the *Yokohama Specie Bank* case, I had issued an order. In the Supreme Court, our advocate, skilled indeed, was asked by one of the Justices (I think it was Frankfurter) whether my order was not arbitrary. I don't think it was at all arbitrary but our advocate did not know the reasons for it and I sat there helplessly hearing our advocate concede that it was an arbitrary decision.

43 *Simenon*: Maigret in Criminal Court p. 76-79 of the French edition. My translation.

44 *Kibosh*: cf. e.g. Partridge, Dictionary of Slang (etc.), McMillan N.Y. 1951, sub voc. Kibosh on, put the, p. 452 sub voc. Kye, p. 464, Partridge is on a better track in his supplement 1961, in the combined 5th edition, p. 1158.

45 *Pisha-paysha:* Rosten, The Joys of Yiddish, McGraw-Hill, 1975, sub. voc. pisha paysha, 288.

45 *Festival of Regrets*: Franklin, The Time of her Life, The New Yorker, April 14, 97, p. 68.

47 *A taste for things that make money*: cf. second chapter, Learning, 232-233.

48 See Stobbrich, this chapter, supra.

49 *I mistakenly believed our family was poor*: See first chapter of this book, Starting, p. 57 and notes pp. 117-118.

50 *Gabe*: Gabe's autobiography, Gabriel Blows his Horn, p. 8.

51 *Annual family picture*: see for example first chapter, Starting, p. 149. This picture was taken after my grandparents had died. My brother and I were away; Irv, I think, studing painting at the Beaux-Arts; I working for Jules Goebel.

⁵² *Galanterie*: Notions. See first chapter of this book, Starting, 54-56.

⁵³ *Partner*: Cf. first chapter of this book, Starting, 58 and note p. 119.

⁵⁴ *Freide Leah's directness*: cf. first chapter of this book, Starting, p. 57.

⁵⁵ *American Red Cross*: When Al Qaeda's suicide bombers hit the World Trade Center and the Pentagon, the ARC again seems to have misbehaved by accepting contributions not fully used for the purpose for which they were given.

⁵⁶ *Berkshire Hathaway B*: Prospectus, May 8, 1996.

⁵⁷ *Physiography:* A song we sang on field trips, written, I believe, by one of our leaders:

> A most religious science / is physiography
>
> It teaches us reliance / on things no man can see.

⁵⁸ *Susie Perkins*: This occurred when I was working for Jules Goebel. Cf second chapter of this book, Learning, Julius Goebel, Jr., p. 204.

⁵⁹ *Friday group*: Oscar was an economist. He advised the founders of Israel and the government. Abba Eban in his memoirs refers to Oscar as 'our learned economic advisor', Personal Witness (G.P. Putman, N.Y., 1992) 217. He knew well all who were important in Israel. He also advised the government of Indonesia.

Ed was New York Times reporter on fiscal matters, then Counselor to the Office of Management and Budget, then Counselor to the Secretary of Commerce, then again Counselor to OMB.

Lou was a paper manufacturer, then Director of the Congressional Joint Committee on Economics.

Franz is a lawyer, representing, among others, German Banks. He is extremely right-wing and regarded George Bush I as much too left-wing.

60 *Dewey*: Menand, reviewing Westbrook, John Dewey and American Democracy, New York Review (June 25, 1992), 50, 53, citing Dewey, The need for a Recovery of Philosophy, (Boydston ed.) The Middle Works (1899-1925, vol. 10, p. 46), and also referring to Reconstruction in Philosophy (1920) and The Quest for Certainty (1929)

61 *A case I thought I should not lose*: See Long Arm in second chapter, Learning, p. 180.

62 *Free lectures*: See Howe & Libo, How we lived, (Richard Marek, N.Y. 1979) 283ff; Harry Golden in Hutchins Hopgood, The Spirit of the Ghetto (with drawings by Jacob Epstein and Notes by Harry Golden)(Frank & Wgnalls Co., 1902, 1965) 242.

63 *One of his graduates*: see the first chapter of this book, Starting, p.38.

64 *That he married*: see first chapter, Starting, p. 42.

65 *Gabe a socialist when it was dangerous*: Gabe, p. 55-56.

66 *Berkman*: Professor Avrich (private communication) tells me about my uncle Herman meeting on the street another

Berkman friend who asked why he was not at the party to raise money for Berkman, who was in financial straits. Herman replied that he didn't know about the party. Had he known he would certainly have been there and if money was being raised, he would certainly have contributed. He took out some money, gave it to the friend and asked him to get it to Berkman. [I cite this from memory because my poor vision makes it difficult to find documentation.]

67 *Anarchist Voices*: Paul Avrich, Abridged Edition, University Press, Princeton, 1996, 41-42, n. 98, 2-8. Avrich says Luba Stein was an only child. I thought I remembered a son. I am mistaken. There was a young man who was an Art Deco sculptor but no doubt he belonged to another family in the same apartment house. His name, I now think was Pimsleur. How could I have made such a mistake? The only explanation I can offer is my age. We had a piece of his sculpture—either a gift to my sister or we bought it. Luba's son, Mark Benenson, confirms that Luba had no siblings.

68 *Anarchy*: Current Developments in Federal Grant Law, 27 (ABA) Public Contract Newsletter, No. 3, Spring 1992) Anarchy, Totalitarianism, 14-15. "When I heard the investigation [of the explosion of the shuttle] would be in Washington, my immediate reaction was not to do it: I have a principle of not going anywhere near Washington or having to do with government, so my immediate reaction was – how am I gonna get out of this?" Feynman, *What Do YOU Care What Other People Think* 117-154.

69 *The fish stink*: See Starting, p.40

VERSE

Roncevaux

Baron, c'est pitié de vous,
Roland, c'est grand' pitié de vous . . .

    Les hauts monts et les sombres vaux,
    Les ports d'Espagne,
    Ont connu le feu de Durandal
    Ont connu le jeu d'armes de l'arrière garde de
        Charlemagne
    Et les Sarrasins.

Les rochers ont oublié

    Où Olivier a vu venir
    La grande rumeur des Sarrasins,
    Pèse le silence.
    Les rochers muets ont oublié.

    Où choquaient la gent de Marsile le Sarrasin
    Et les bons Francs de la douce France,
    Où coulait à flots le sang vermeil,
    Les eaux murmurent paisiblement.

    Les rochers gris ont oublié.

Roland est mort, et Olivier,
Les douze pairs de la douce France.
Preux et barons, c'est grand' pitié.

Les haut monts et les sombres vaux,
Les ports d'Espagne,
Ont connu le feu de Durandal
(Ce fut l'épée d'un bon vassal)
Ont vu venir la vaste armée des Sarrasins.
Ont ouï hurler le cri d'armes de Charlemagne
Quand choquaient les Francs et les Sarrasins:

    Paiens ont tort et Chrétiens ont droit!
    Aux armes! À cheval! Montjoie!
    Mourront les faux preux du félon roi!
    Mourront qui en Dieu ne croient!
    Pour la douce France et la vraie foi,
    Frappons! Frappons! Montjoie!

    Montjoie!
Les rochers muets ont oublié.

Roland est mort, et Olivier,
Les douze pairs de la douce France,
Preux et barons, c'est grand' pitié.

    Sonnez toujours l'oliphant.
    Sonnez toujours le cor.   Roland
        Est mort.

                [juin 1929?]

translated August 24, 2002

    Roncevaux

Baron, we have pity for you
Roland, we have much pity for you.

The high mountains and the dark valleys
the gates of Spain,
have known the fire of Durandal,
have known the clash of arms of the rear guard of
    Charlemagne
and the Sarrasins.

The rocks have forgotten.

Where Oliver saw the great mass
of the Sarrasins arrive
Silence weighs.
The quiet rocks have forgotten.

Where the army of Marsile the Sarrasin
Clashed with the good Franks of sweet France,
Where the red blood flowed
The waters now murmur peacefully,
The gray rocks have forgotten.

Roland has died and Oliver,
The twelve peers of sweet France.
Knights and barons, we have pity for you.

The high mountains and the dark valleys,
The gates of Spain
Have known the fire of Durandal
(It was the sword of a good vassal)
Have seen the vast crowd of the Sarrasins arrive
Have heard shout the cry at arms of Charlemagne
When the Franks clashed with the Sarrasins:

> Pagans are wrong. Christians are right!
> To arms! To horse! Montjoie!
> The false knights of the felon king will die!
> They who do not believe in God will die!

> For sweet France and the true faith
> Let us strike! Strike! Montjoie!
>
>> Montjoie!
>
> The silent rocks have forgotten.
>
> Roland, has died, and Oliver,
> The twelve peers of sweet France
> Knights and Barons, we pity you.
>
>> Let the trumpet always sound
>> Let the horn blow.   Roland
>>   is dead.

* * *

Je souffre . . . en mon âme je souffre, à cause de la faiblesse,
À cause de la corruption de l'esprit des hommes—
Je hais toute mollesse.
J'ai soif d'une boisson   âcre!
Satan! depuis que j'ai goûté la vendange noire de vos vignes
Je suis altéré . . . je souffre . . .
En mon âme je souffre, à cause de la faiblesse!

Je crie dans mon angoisse, Maudits, les esprits courbés!—
Maudit que je suis car mon esprit est courbé!
J'ai soif d'une boisson   âcre!

Satan! c'est votre superbe,
Satan, c'est votre calme hautain, et dédaigneux.
Mal! c'est votre roideur, qu'il me faut—
Et je crie dans mon angoisse.

[Juin 1929]

translated August 24, 2002

I suffer . . . in my soul, I suffer because of weakness
Because of the corruption of the soul of men
I hate all softness
I thirst for drink that's   bitter
Satan! since I have tasted the black pressing of your vines
I thirst   I suffer
In my soul I suffer because of weakness!

I cry in my anguish, Damned be the bent souls!
Damned that I am   for my soul is bent!
I thirst for drink that's   bitter

Satan! it is your pride
Satan! it is your high and disdainful calm.
Evil, it is your severity that I need . . .
And I cry in my anguish

Winter

has come suddenly this year.
There   were   warm days
and then   the trees
were   in the first frost   bare.
                                    [June 1929]

River bank in Spring

The willows are curious twists of gray,
half-seen through green
—and yellow mists.
                                    [June 1929]

Two Haiku

The wind is only
Something that sets your face out
In front of your ears.

This office chair stands
With legs apart, with back arched,
Its fists on its hips.

[June 1929]

There are even large moons
citron staring
salmon intricated clouds
and blue mist

and slow horses in pairs
drinking water

and birch lines
leaning out of the hill mist

[Westfield, Christmas, 1931]

long lines of trains
with smoke at the end

and trees like smoke
at the end of long lines of trees

and shallow dark water
like trees

[Becket, New York, 1932]

There is the low dark remembering of hair
of words that lie like smoke on mountain paths
The low dark ringing of the burning air
and I remember now a lost remembering
of something

                                          [1932]

(Edith):
There is a moment at the edge of stairs
when *swell*ing in unbalance like a wave
plunge slowly

                                          [1932]

I want to learn   how living is done

                                    [July, 1932]

These leaves going perfectly,
       wholly done with trees
(But only when a wind comes
       such as this)
who drily joyous race
and stop when
such a wind as this says stop

                                    [Nov 1, 1934]

Lachrimae Rerum

Triste! . . . que le monde est beau . . .

Les parfums suaves, doux
—La délicate odeur des blanches fleurs d'avril—
Évanouiront bientôt.

Triste, la lumière!

Les couleurs riches, gaies,
—Le feuillage en soleil, hélas—
Sont éphémères.
                Ah, Dieu!

La belle lumière!

Triste, le chant des oiseaux
Le matin, dans le bois—
La saveur des fruits—
Le frôlement de la soie—
Triste, que le monde est beau!

Ah! que la vie est triste . . .
Puisque ma chère m'est douce,
Puisque le monde est cher,
Puisque nous sommes tous, hélas,
Éphémères . . .
                Ah, Dieu!
Que la vie est triste . . .
Que le monde est cher . . .

Que la vie est triste . . .
Puisque nous sommes tous, hélas,
Éphémères! . . . .

                                      [1931]

translated August 24, 2002

It is sad! that the world is fine . . .

Perfumes sweet and soft
—The delicate odor of white flowers of April—
will vanish soon.
Sad, that the world is fine!

Sad, the light!
The colors rich and gay
—The leafage in the sun, alas—
are ephemeral.
        Oh, God!

The beautiful light!

Sad, the song of the birds,
In the morning in the woods—
The taste of fruits—
The rustle of silk—
Sad, that the world is fine!

Ah, how sad is life . . .
Because my dear is kind,
Because the world is dear,
Because we are all, alas,
Ephemeral . . .
        Oh, God!

How sad is life . . .
How dear is the world . . .

How sad is life . . .
Because we are all, alas,
Ephemeral! . . . .

* * *

The sky is hard.

Only a Titan can
Smash! the sky.
Only a mighty fist can
Shatter! the sky,
Rock! the earth,
Throttle! the sun.
Only the fire of a mighty wrath can
Burn! the sky.

What eye has sufficient power
To make *these* trees shudder?
What voice has clear authority
To make *these* trees cower?
What forge has heat sufficient—
What smith has strength to hammer
The iron speartips of this Titan's anger.

Has God courage,
And has earth armor,
To defy this fury? . . .
Has man courage,
Has man armor,
To dare to look upon this glory? . . .

Has man the will to utterly destroy?
Has man heart to batter at and shatter
All foundations? . . .

Hell! only,
Only the unquenchable fire, now
Is wild enough . . . .

Not even Hell is adequate to the pain
Of the slow pity of this rain . . . .

Night . . . only,
Only the inextinguishable black, now,
Is impersonal enough . . . .

[1929?]

    There is a certain elm tree in a Berkshire meadow, where the wind blows all day and all night from the northwest, whipping the branches to the southeast.
    And seen from the west, or the southwest, or the south, there is a tension in its asymmetry that makes me taut and my vision cleaner.

[Becket, Sept. 1927]

The true value of walking is that it is after all a kind of sleep.
    And the leaves and flowers, the bird sounds and the wood smells that come to us, walking, are after all a kind of dream, and dusted over with the dust of dreams.

[Raquette Lake, Sept. '29]

And yet her hair was singing in the rain light
The morning of the lost and longing eyes
How happy hands wave in the morning
And her hair was brighter than the days.

How often hands wave without greeting
(Her ring that rounds on stone)
And yet her hair was singing
Where the ring's rose
Was blood and tears and gold.

[1929]

Questions pour Lazare de Béthanie

Lazare, à quoi pensiez-vous là-bas, Lazare
Vous souveniez-vous de la vie, Lazare
Lazare, vous rappeliez-vous le jour

À quoi pensiez-vous là-bas, Lazare
À la blanche clarté du jour
À la douce chaleur
Nu sur la montagne
Empoignant le vent
courant le soleil
Raide est la montagne
son geste tendu
Nu! la poitrine
qui hurle! la montagne
Son geste tendu
Nu! le vent
mort nu tendu tombeau

Lazare, affreux visage vu là-bas
affres du vent gouffres à quoi
qui hurle! la montagne
à quoi pensiez-vous là-bas, Lazare
aux promenades matinales dans la forêt
et la verte odeur
la lente lutte des arbres
que le sol sait, riche de feuilles
que la paix, de feuilles
que la peine
que le sol heureux de feuilles
sait que feuilles
que la paix que mort des arbres
et la verte odeur
beau visage vu là-bas, Lazare
que le sol sait

Nu!
la lente lutte des arbres
Nu! les jambes
le geste tendu
Nu! la poitrine
que le sol sait
que la paix que mort des arbres
et la verte odeur
beau visage vu là-bas,
Lazare,
Dans le tombeau
vous souveniez-vous de la forêt
Dans le cerceuil
vous rappeliez-vous la verte odeur
Dans le silence
Vous rappeliez-vous le chant
Dans le froid
vous souveniez-vous de la chaleur

Dans la nuit
vous rappeliez-vous le jour

À quoi pensiez-vous là-bas, Lazare
affres du vent gouffres à quoi
qui hurle! la montagne
et la verte odeur
Raide est la montagne
que la paix que mort des arbres
seul le vent soupire encore
seule la lune peut voir
Nu!
la lente lutte des arbres
et dans l'ombre meurent les feuilles
seul le vent soupire encore
que la paix que mort des arbres
et la verte odeur

Lazare
Dans la nuit
Vous rappeliez-vous le jour

Lazare, à quoi pensiez-vous là-bas
Vous souveniez-vous de la vie, Lazare
Vous rappeliez-vous le jour, Lazare

Lazare, vous rappeliez-vous la nuit
Lazare, vous souveniez-vous de la mort.

[le premier août, 1931]

translated August 24, 2002

Questions for Lazarus of Bethany

Lazarus, what were you thinking of down there, Lazarus
Were you remembering life, Lazarus
Lazarus, did you recall the day

What did you think about, down there, Lazarus
Of the white clarity of the day
Of the soft warmth
Naked on the mountain
Grasping the wind
running the sun
Rigid is the mountain
its gesture strained
Naked! the legs
Stiff is the mountain
Naked! the chest
who shouts! the mountain
its gesture stretched
Naked! the wind
dead naked stretched tomb

Lazarus, frightful visage seen down there
horrors of wind chasms to which
who shouts! the mountain
what were you thinking of, down there, Lazarus
of morning walks in the forest
and its green smell
the slow struggle of trees
that the earth knows, rich in leaves
that the peace, of leaves
that the pain
that the earth happy of leaves
knows that leaves
that the peace that death of trees
and its green smell

fine visage seen down there, Lazarus
that the earth knows
Naked!
the slow struggle of the trees
Naked! the legs
the strained gesture
Naked! the chest
that the earth knows
that the peace that death of trees
and the green smell
handsome face seen down there
Lazarus,
In the tomb
did you remember the woods
In the coffin
did you recall the green smell
In the silence
did you recall the song
In the cold
did you remember the warmth

In the night
Did you recall the day

What did you think about down there, Lazarus
Horrors of wind chasms to which
who shouts! the mountain
and the green smell
Stiff, the mountain
that the peace that death of trees
only the wind still breathes
only the moon can see
Naked!
the slow struggle of the trees
and in the shadow die the leaves
only the wind still breathes
that the peace that death of trees
and the green smell

Lazarus
In the night
Did you recall the day

Lazarus, what did you think about down there
Did you remember life, Lazarus
Did you recall the day

Lazarus, did you recall the night
Lazarus, did you remember death

   * * *

My desire is not upon the mountains
Where it flows
There is no other fortune in designing
'Brocade and stiff brocade and stiff parade'

Nor any other wind blows
Where the twining
Of the ancient river goes.

This is the end torch of my burning
And the breasts of my declining
And the dragon of my writhing
And the breath.

There is no mountain singing
Nor any wind blows
Where the marching
Cries the ancient death.

[1930]

Ce n'est pas sur les montagnes,
mon désir,
Ni y a-t-il d'autre fortune à dessiner
là où il coule
Ni y a-t-il d'autre vent qui souffle
là où va la sinuosité
de la rivière ancienne

Voici le fin feu de mon martyre
Voici les seins de mon abaissement
Voici le serpent de mon agonie
Voici le souffle

Il n'y a pas de montagne qui chante
Ni aucun vent ne souffle
là où la marche proclame
la mort ancienne.

[Grenoble, juin 1931]

Translations from Horace

I-XI
      Tu ne quaesieris

Ne cherchez pas, Leuconoé.   Il ne faut pas savoir
Combien de jours nous sont donnés. Ne tentez pas les nombres
Babyloniens, qu'on nous accorde plusieurs années, que cet
hiver soit le dernier, mieux vaut se soumettre . . . et boire.

La vie est courte, que les espoirs   soient courts. Profitez
du jour, on ne peut rien savoir   du lendemain. Le temps coule
pendant que nous parlons . . . . Versez à boire!

Sur la côte Toscane la mer noire   se brise contre les rochers

II-XIV
      Eheu! fugaces . . .

Postumus, Postumus, les années passent.
Hélas,   nulle sacrifice
n'arrête la mort.
ni l'or   ni les pierres précieuses
n'achètent exemption.
Pluton enfin nous reçoit
tous, rois et bergers.

Postumus, Postumus, les années passent,
Hélas,   il faudra quitter
terre et foyer et femme.
La flamme   noire du seul cyprès
Toi trépassé, se souviendra de toi.
Et versera   ton vin un héritier plus digne.
—L'insigne cécube, gardé sous cent clefs.

Postumus, Postumus, les années passent.

[juin 1931]

Englished August 24, 2002

Tu ne quaesieris

Seek not, Leuconoe. It is not needful to know
How many days we are given. Do not try the Babylonian
Numbers. Whether we have several years
or whether this winter is the last
      it is better to submit
           and drink

Life is short. Let our hopes   be short . . . Capture
the day. We cannot know anything of tomorrow. Time flows
even as we speak.   Pour us to drink!

On the Tuscan coast the black sea breaks against the rocks.

    Eheu! fugaces . . .

Postumus, Postumus, the years pass.
Alas,   no sacrifice
can halt   death.
no gold   no precious stones
can buy   exemption.
Pluto at last receives us
all, kings and shepherds
Postumus, Postumus, the years pass,

Alas,   we must yield
field and hearth and wife
the black fire   of the single cypress alone
when you are gone will remember you.
And an inheritor   more worthy will pour the wine
—the fine cecuba, kept under a hundred locks

Postumus, Postumus,   the years pass.

Dear Virginia

The planned exurban community is not fertilized
by the chance encounter, by the mind surprised.

Birds *not* of a feather
ought to flock together.

The Wall Street broker
needs to meet the joker from Madison Ave.
                The Madison Aver
needs to palaver
with the Columbia prof.   The professor's a fellow
who needs the bordello.
The Madame is fond of soyed fish at Wu's
        and Wu plays poker
every Tuesday with the broker.

Thus, their centrifugal tendencies
are nicely balanced by centripetal energies
to the great advantage of their creativity.
To decentralize them would be a pity.

The broker's daughter has a (Russian) music tutor

whose son-in-law is a cloak-and-suiter.
The cloak-and-suiter's luncheon waiter
goes on Mondays to a doctor who's a speculator
in West Side apartments. His (Swedish) superintendent
is named co-respondent
in a messy divorce by the little Boston mouse
who is Senior Partner in the broker's investment house

The stirring of this chowder pot
brings each a whiff of something he has not.

The country for serenity
The suburbs for amenity
But the city
for serendipity.

[1951]

[My sister Bryna had gone to Israel for a meeting of Hadassah. This was written to greet her on her return. It takes off from a sonnet by DuBellay (1525-1560)(Les Regrets, Sonnet XXXI). The strange spellings of the French are based on spellings of DuBellay's time. Esther is another name for Hadassah.]

Heureux qui, comme Ulysse, a fait un beau voyage
A travers des mers jusqu'au lointain rivage
Pour voir les monuments que le temps a dontez
Et les viex murs du Temple que l'herbe a surmontez

Les theatres en rond ouvers de tous costez
Le hopital nouveau qu'Hadassah a fondez
Sacrez costaux et sainctes ruines du temps biblique
Et la presse d'un peuple moderne et energique

Il fait bon voir (Esther) un conclave serre

En un petit recoign de dix pieds en carre
Etudier l'avenir de l'Ecole de Medecine

Il fait bon voir dehors toute la ville en foire
Crier l'un a l'aultre, voisin a sa voisine:
Hadassah a votez un nouveau laboratoire.

[7 fevrier 1971]

translated August 24, 2002

Happy, who like Ulysses, has made a fine voyage
across the seas to distant shores
to see the monuments that have succumbed to the years
and the old walls covered with grass

The round theaters open on all sides
the new hospital that Hadassah has founded
Sacred hills and holy ruins of biblical days
and the crowds of modern and energetic people

It is good (Esther) to see a crowded conclave
meet in a little room, ten feet square
to study the future of the School of Medicine

It is good to see outdoors the village all in fair
cry one to another, neighbor to neighbor:
Hadassah has voted a new lab.

Maragon

Sold, said the cobweb to the flying machine,
Ain't no way we're gonna get this falarumtum clean.
Cut out your corribles and satisfy your mulligan,
You're gonna have to vegetate, I attapulgite mean.

Soft, said the hooligan, it's getting kind of horrible,
There ain't no living way we're gonna sablifigan green.
We're oyster over the living board,
We're feather the winsome gravy gourd,
We're ever many the vineyard in the night of our lateen.

Salute the vigor of the fire,
Vicissitudes of open dale,
A brithero'some in the mire
Of calsifortitudinous hail.
We're over the seas and back again,
A crepitude of the roiling stain,
In the astral trace of the culsimore.
You'll have to go home in the winding rain.

Sir, said the flyer to the cobious machine,
Ain't no way you're gonna get the finial careen.
Cut short collectibles and stubble your martingale,
We'll allocate the overforce and concentrate the queen.

[January 16, 1987]

Ad mirandum

O recidivist in the algebraic sense, how came you home?
what voyage of the vicious subalert has grown
to muck the stall of all the nation's hurt?
Immense confusion of the aching heart
can hardly tot up those reverberations.   Go.

[January 30, 1987]

Let us not, the poet asks
subordinate our daily tasks
to empty dreams.
We are not gods
        We cannot make a world from nought.
let us just list the things we ought
to do, and leave to gods
        the larger themes.

[March 30, 1992]

The Lost Dutchman Gold Mine

My name is Jacob Waltz,
And while I have my faults,
I found the richest gold mine in the Superstition Hills.

The gold is there, all right,
But I hid it out of sight.
I'd point it out to you, but right now I've got the chills.

I'm an accommodating chap.
I made a little map.
But topographic drawing is not one of my skills.

With a shovel and a pick,
It's covered pretty slick
And the only way to find it is to follow this here line.

Don't imagine that I'm drunk.
Just look thar in my trunk.
It's full of the richest ore, and it's mine—all mine.

I feel I'm getting cold,
But before I fold,
I've got to tell *some*one about the Dutchman's Mine.

Put a blanket on my bed,
And a pillow under my head,
And give me a gulp of whuskey for I'm tight around the gills.

Oh, my name is Jacob Waltz,
And while I have my faults,
I found the richest gold mine in the Superstition Hills.

THAT IS ALL HE SAID.

THESE ARE THE LAST WORDS OF JACOB WALTZ,
RECORDED BY MALCOLM S. MASON

>Mesa, Arizona
[February 21, 1992]

>Particulate the memory
>open hope and rust
>clarifies the homily
>rarifies the dust
and lo, telephone, on the way to a tree
>>mankind cannot adjust
mystery woman from out of the sea
>>gabardine covered with must

>>[1969?]

[The following verse is by Irma. It is intended to reflect a telephone conversation she had with our daughter.

The broken rhyme (thumb-umb-rage) was a favorite device of Irma's.]

Doggerel for Mother dear

You can't give me anything but Mazeltov, Mother—
That's the only thing I want from your love, Mother

Twenty three I will be,
    Not a child, as you must see.
Fully grown, on my own,
    Facing up to all I've sown.
Have no care, just be there
    If and when I've time to spare.
Do not cry, nor yet sigh
    You'll see baby—by and by.
Don't be bright, say I'm right
    Cheer me up with all your might.
Don't be sad—good or bad.
    Tell your baby you are glad.
Love me well, but don't tell
    Anything that's hard or fell.
Chew the rag, wave a flag,
    I know what is my right bag.
Be no fool, play it cool
    Even if I seem part mule.
Keep on keel what you feel,
    Mazeltov, Mother, is your spiel.
Have no fear, shed no tear
    Mazeltov only, Mother dear.

So—
Don't be a mourner
Stay in your corner
Like little Jack Horner, Mother dear.
Don't put in your thumb
For I will take umb—
            rage, Mother dear.

You'll have to rough it.
Sit on your tuffet
Like little Miss Muffet, Mother dear.
Eating curds and whey
Without words—I may
     be frightened, Mother dear.

Doggerel for Daughter dear

I can't give you anything but Mazeltov, baby—
That's the only thing you want from my love, baby

Twenty three you'll soon be,
  Not a child, as I do see.
Almost grown, on your own,
  Coping well with what you've sown.

At your age and your stage
  Life is open, page by page.
It is true you can do
  As you like, for good or rue.
With your sight you must write—
  Don't deprive yourself of light.

Twenty one—by law, done—
  You were mostly seeking fun.
At that age, not too sage
  You were still engrossed in rage.

Now at last has the past
  In its proper place been cast?
Are you now sure of how
  Not to childish fancies bow?

Are you able and/or stable
    Enough to know fact from fable?
Has life taught how to sort—
    Separate the "is" from "ought"?
Are you free so as to see
    Which is forest, which a tree?
And find out, without doubt,
    What it is you're all about?

Don't be meek—you're not weak,
    You must find the life you seek.
Do not fear—get it clear—
    What it is you hold most dear.

Though I'm square—still, ta mère,
Hoping that your life be fair.
Though I'm flip—and a drip,
All good wishes for your trip.

                                        [1969]

    The following lines are by Jan, our daughter.

To my Father

Why do I praise the Lord?
What do I mean by it?
    I mean I praise being able, not fearful
    I praise rescue from abandonment
    I praise becoming free, no longer in a trap
Yet I also praise the abandonment that makes the rescue sweet,
And the trap that when opened makes us long to see others free.
    I praise being given a hand
    And I praise giving a hand.
So do we not worship at the same mount, father,
    Do we not drink from the same fount?

My Abombinable Autobiography

MY ABOMBINABLE AUTOBIOGRAPHY

Hand to hand
Sausage to Caesar
The power of the Atom
So are we all
$_{92}U^{238}$
> About 1903, my father performed an early, perhaps (as he believed) the first commercial quantitative analysis of uranium ore.

Oppy
> About 1921, my sister Bryna was a classmate at Ethical Culture High School of Robert Oppenheimer.

Chemistry
My Three Mile Island
Einstein
dx/dy
D_2O
Executive Privilege
Government secrecy
Mike
> Michael was born April 3, 1945. The first A-bomb dropped in anger was Hiroshima, August 6, 1945.

How
Alamogordo
Oak Ridge
Saratoga

Coffee
> When I went to Brussels from Paris in 1947, the train served coffee made of acorns. Once the train crossed the border into Belgium, the same dining car served real coffee. The reason was the Belgian Congo had Uranium and Belgium was therefore rich.

Heavy Water
OSS
OAP
AEP
Shelter
ER
City Bar
> About 1962, I was a member of the Atomic Energy Law Committee of the Bar Association of the City of New York.

Mid-Continent
> About 1960, I was a director of Mid-Continent Uranium Corporation (Colorado).

AEC
> About 1965, I wrote a paper on the deficiencies of the Atomic Energy Commission.

SALT
Space
Hiroshima
Irwin's Party
SEC staff dinner
The Hard Way to Peace
> Irma and I helped Bob Clampitt arrange a series of seminars on nuclear arms and nuclear power, based in part on Etzioni's book, The Hard Way to Peace [1962]

FBA—Committee on Federal Grants
> As a major undertaking of the Committee, I drafted and the Committee approved an Outline on the Use of Grants in the Energy Field.

My Abombinable Autobiography

5/1/92

The eras we live in may be defined by their most influential developments, in popular use if not in invention. These overlap very much, of course. Taking a span of about five generations—our granddaughters Sharan and Amber, our children, Mike and Jan, Irma and me, Pop and Rae, my grandparents Aaron and Freida Leah, Abe and Mollie—about 150 years, these include on the hardware side, for my grandchildren, space flights, camcorders and VCR's; for my children, rockets, computers, television, photocopying; for Irma and me, the atom bomb and atom power, airplanes, tape recorders, radio, automobiles, moving pictures; for my parents, telephone, electric light, electric motors, dynamos, x-ray; for my grandparents, steam ships, railroads, photography.

On the software side, we may note among others, von Neumann, game theory; Turing, symbolic logic and computer theory; Watkins, DNA; Einstein, relativity and quantum theory; Hubble and the exploding universe; Freud, psycho-analysis and the sexual revolution; Darwin, evolution and materialism. There are of course many others that could be named. This is one selection.

3/14/01

In family life, lessons we might learn from our parents' failures or from their successes are not likely to be sound because the world meanwhile has always changed. My parents were born and spent their pre-teen years in an anti-Semitic and authoritarian Europe. They came to live in America where they had to acquire a culture wholly new to them. When they were born it was a horse-drawn world. When I was born automobiles were rapidly becoming a commonplace and airplanes an interesting novelty. My uncle George selected wood for airplane propellers. My uncle Chuck trained as an airplane artillery spotter. I think I first crossed the Atlantic by plane in 1951 after Mike and Jan were born. My parents knew about telephones. I knew about radio. Mike and Jan know about atomic bomb threats, television, computers, the Internet. Each generation was wildly different. These are hardware matters. But they carry software implications and the software changes are even more striking.

Some random examples out of many. When I left government in 1950, government would not dream of supporting family planning. Single women with children were few and not talked about. When I came back to government in 1966, my secretary was very openly a single mother and it was very common not only in Hollywood but in Washington. She felt that as a single mother she had a *right* to spend hours of her workday on the telephone to monitor her latch key kids. Family planning was no longer unthinkable it had become a mandatory part of government support programs. Today, the point of controversy is not contraception but abortion and not really abortion but disposal of aborted fetuses. In the 1940s, drive-by shootings, kids mowing down classmates were not part of the world spirit. Strip shows were well known but not respectable. Today, Naked News is available free on the Internet. These are not important but symptoms of thoroughgoing fast change. Whatever lessons my parents learned or I learned from their successes or failures hardly fit the new world we lived in after Mike and Jan were born. There were new problems, new expectations, new rules of life. What had been unthinkable became common place. I don't know what Nietsche meant, but there has certainly been a transvaluation of values.

Housing and eating places were segregated. In 1938 in Washington, I had to search for a restaurant where a black lawyer and I could eat together. Jewish parents in Europe grew up with deep respect for *their* parents. Immigrant Jews in America often (not always, not, I believe in our family, but it was not unusual) grew up ashamed of *their* parents who did not understand English and the American culture. The generation after that did not grow up with disrespect but could no longer reflect the deep respect of two generations back. Talmudic scholars came here and earned a living by carrying enormous back loads of cut cloth to sewing sweatshops. A generation later German law professors came here as refugees and got jobs as waiters. Concert pianists, if they were lucky, got jobs accompanying camp songs at Greylock.

What is the parenting job for black parents whose kids now grow up seeing that selling drugs and pimping and joining murderous gangs is the quickest road to unbelievable riches and community "respect", unless you are tall and quick on your feet. They can tell their kids to go to church, work hard to get a good schooling. Will the kids take them seriously. Nah. People like Mattie, our longtime housekeeper, if they become parents, have the right qualities but it won't work for them. How ya gonna keep 'em down on the farm after they've seen Paree? How do you grow good decent kids in black communities who have seen the payoff for lying and demagoguery for Clayton Powell, Al Sharpton, Farrakhan and the drug lords, pimps, and gang leaders?

In a rapidly changing world, the job of being a good parent is difficult, close to impossible. That does not mean we should not try our best to learn.

5/1/92

Hand to hand

Those who have lived in a time of some great development, although they have not contributed to the development or participated in it, if they think persistently about it will nevertheless find that they have many nerves of connection to the theme of their time. If this were not so, it would not be an era-defining development. We are all connected to our time, as we are all connected to our world. It is said, I think correctly, that anyone, however private, could find among his relations someone whose relations and their relations within a small number of steps could connect him with any other person in the world, however great, or low, or remote. I know someone who knows someone who knows someone who knows the Secretary of the Communist Party in China, or a beggar in Madras, and I know someone who knows someone who built the atomic bomb, and probably someone who knows someone who knows someone who knows someone killed at Hiroshima. So, if you search, do you, I think.

Sausage to Caesar

How significant are these connections? Tracing connections not too obvious but not too trivial and not verbalistic is an old game of mine. Irma enjoyed challenging me to connect any two ideas of her choice. What is the connection of sausage to Caesar? (Don't tell me you eat Caesar salad and sausages). Although it is not difficult, the neatness of the answer pleased her and it became a favorite of hers. She often talked about sausage to Caesar. Caesar died and turned to dust, out of which grew plants edible to swine who would be made into sausage.

> Imperious Caesar dead and turned to clay
> Might stop a hole to keep the wind away
> Or feed the roots of oak and beech to furnish
> Mast that will wild forest hogs then nourish.

[The first two lines are from Edward DeVere's Hamlet, Act V, Scene i, line 232. The second two are Bacon's.]

The power of the Atom

Let us consider the atom, whose power was dimly seen before I was born and may destroy us all by the time I finish and which surely defines the era we live in.   I was not an atomic scientist nor a politician involved in encouraging or hindering the creation of the bomb or its use. Yet, on giving thought, I find many paths that connect me with it. I will list some of them. Some, it is true, are slight. Most may seem trivial, but I have these connections and they are meaningful to me. Much of my life could be narrated, focusing on these threads of connection. I think anyone else of my generation who may at first think himself unconnected could find such threads, giving thought to it.

So are we all

Of course, in a broad sense, every living person has been affected by the bomb. It ended the War in a way that otherwise might not have happened. It would have ended the War differently if the Germans had successfully built it first, or if Harry Truman had decided not to drop it. But I am looking for more personal connections.

$$_{92}U^{238}$$

About 1903, my father performed an early, perhaps (as he believed) the first commercial quantitative analysis of uranium ore. Uranium was discovered in 1789 in Saxony pitchblende. In 1841, the metal was first extracted from UO_2. In 1869, Mendeleev formulated the periodic system. Uranium was then the element with the heaviest known atomic weight. The first transuranium elements were discovered in 1940 (neptunium and plutonium). That is something I remember reading about in the newspaper. In 1896, Becquerel discovered the radioactivity of uranium.

Uranium was used commercially in tungsten lamps as an anti-surge buffer; in ceramic glazes; as a textile mordant to fix dyes; and in special steels. Other uses were experimented with.

A leading refiner of uranium bought a shipment of uranium ore that it believed was not up to the warranty specifications. Pop was a chemist before he was a physician and ran a commercial laboratory (which he continued for many years after he became a physician—perhaps to 1930 approximately). The refiner asked Pop whether he could test the shipment. Pop said, "Of course". He then turned to the books and found that no one seemed to have done quantitative analysis of uranium ore and no one had described a procedure. He decided that if he replicated in his laboratory the complicated process used in commercial extraction of uranium, his results ought to be only more accurate. He did this three times and averaged the results and concluded that the shipment was below grade. He testified in court as to his qualifications and his results and (probably) was cross-examined on his methods. I believe his client won. About 50 years later, Pop died of cancer. Is that related to his exposure to uranium at a time when the dangers were not yet fully known? Probably not or probably, at most, a little. Bryna and Irv and my cousins Lucy and David also died of cancers. As for me, we don't know yet. (I am not suggesting a connection.)

Oppy

About 1921, my sister Bryna was a classmate at Ethical Culture High School of Robert Oppenheimer.

Oppenheimer had mathematical brilliance, ability to manage a large project, and humanistic ethics. His mathematical brilliance, of course, did not come from Ethical's teaching, but it is possible that it was encouraged by Ethical's approach to mathematics, which emphasized, in geometry for example, intuition of relationships more than rigor of proof. Bryna, while never a mathematical genius, did develop the sense of how things ought to be. While Ethical did not *give* this to Oppenheimer, it may have encouraged it or at least did not discourage it. In contrast, my high school mathematics emphasized rigor of proof. I was gifted in that and applied it later in symbolic logic, but less gifted in "seeing" the relationships. When I read Bryna's geometry book, probably 3 or 4 years later, I was inclined to sneer at the under-emphasis on rigor. Later, however, I became convinced that the great mathematical physicists *see* first and try to prove later if at all. I am a devotee of rigor of proof. Ethical was not and the great physicists Einstein, Oppenheimer, Feynman were not. Gell-Mann's work on "the 8-fold way" sub-atomic particles is an example. Einstein is an outstanding example. The algebra in his theory of relativity was originally faulty. When this was pointed out, he acknowledged it and corrected it, but he never had any doubt that his results were sound.

My friend Raoul Berger cherishes a letter from Einstein to Raoul's father-in-law, Dr. Beck, in which Einstein acknowledges in an entirely different context, a faulty decimal place. Einstein sitting with Dr. Beck around beers (in Berlin), had said it would be easy for Germany to pay the World War I Reparations. There were in Germany X Museums. Each had on an average Y Rembrants. Each Rembrant was worth on an average Z gold Marks. X x Y x Z comes to more than the Reparations the Allies demanded. The next day he wrote to say, We must have had more beers than I thought; my arithmetic was wrong.

Oppenheimer's ability to see the whole scope of a complex project and to break it up into manageable parts in an organized way, was, I believe, definitely aided by Ethical's teaching. In a lesser way, it was something that Bryna had that was taught or reinforced by Ethical. It was reflected in Bryna's managing (and teaching Irma and me to manage) Camp, and in preparing management guides for the Hospital, and in conducting the Hadassah "Large Gifts" program, and in the purposeful management of her own remaining life when she was told, correctly, that she had six months to live.

Oppenheimer's humanistic ethics, reflected in his deep concern about the human consequences of using the bomb he had created, was surely conferred or encouraged by Ethical. It was reflected in Bryna's personality too.

Chemistry

As noted earlier, about 1924, although I was an excellent student of chemistry at Evander Childs H.S. (then on Creston Avenue, Bronx), my refusal to keep a notebook got me the "punishment" of a failing grade at midterm "to teach me a lesson". At the same time, for the same reason, I got a failing grade in biology. (At the same time, I also got a failing grade in French because I corrected my teacher's pronunciation.) Neither in college nor in law school have I kept notes, which I considered useless and contrary to my ways of learning, nor in Philosophy class in France where Professor Chevalier not only told us to keep notebooks but told us what to put on the left side of the page (the comments he underlined to be cherished for their deep significance) and what on the right hand side (an ordinary summary of his remarks). [Years later, about 35 years later, I found a law school professor at Aix teaching in the same spirit. He had taught, as a visitor, at Cornell and I chided him on this teaching style. He said he didn't like it but his students wanted it.]

I dropped chemistry and biology and refused to retract when both chemistry and biology instructors begged me to do so because they knew I was their best student and they had hoped only to jar me. Perhaps I would have gone on to work in atomic chemistry if I had not been so stubborn. Perhaps. Whistler flunked out of West Point. He said, "If silicon had been a gas, I would have been a general." I knew that silicon was not a gas at ordinary temperatures but was unwilling to write that in a notebook just because other students needed that crutch.

My Three Mile Island

About that time (1924), I visited my father's uptown lab on Jerome Avenue. He probably still had his downtown lab on 124th Street where he had moved from the Horton Building on 125th Street next door to a large department store (Alexander's). He had to be out for a short time. I asked permission to set up apparatus to generate oxygen, Do you know how? Oh, yes. You put a very small piece of sodium in a retort of water and lead off the oxygen through a tube into a bottle inverted in water. OK. (This was book learning but it was reasonable to believe I knew what I was doing.) I grossly misjudged what was a "very small" piece of sodium and had an explosion. Pop returned soon after. He checked me for injuries and then set about helping me clean up the wreckage. I was never scolded for the accident. After cleaning up, Pop asked how large was the piece of sodium. About the size of my little finger nail. It should have been about the size of a pin head.

Einstein

About 1924 (the date is uncertain, but I was a young teenager), I read somewhere (New York Times? Popular Science??) that a scientist at one of the Universities would send a free copy of Einstein's latest paper to anyone requesting it. I sent for it, received it, "read it" but did not understand it. I did not have any vector analysis. I enjoyed it for its music not its sense. Today, I still read science for music—the statement of themes, the rhythm of the connections of ideas, the bridge passages, the developments, the recapitulations, and codas. *Scientific American*, is for me, more accessible than the more serious journals like *Science* or *Nature*. I don't recall what paper of Einstein's this was. I think of it as related to unified field theory, but if I remember the year correctly, it was more likely his paper on monoatomic gases.

dx/dy

About 1927, my calculus professor at Columbia (I had also had calculus in high school) was Koopman who was a great mathematician and later worked on the bomb project. I never learned enough of differential equations and vector analysis or tensors to get into that field.

D_2O

About 1929, I had a friend at Columbia whose name I have forgotten who said his special field of interest was atomic physics. (I connect him with Milton Katims. Can it be? Why not? If Einstein played the fiddle why couldn't a violist study atomic physics?) I did not know what that meant and somehow did not have the curiosity to probe. I find this surprising because I had lots of curiosity. Perhaps I mistakenly thought I knew what he meant and mistakenly thought it was not important. Perhaps he was working with Urey. I had heard something of Urey's work with heavy water. I was startled—but this was probably later—by the story of Urey's drinking a glass of it. Urey was at Columbia about 1929 to the 1940s. He got the Nobel Prize in 1934 for discovery of heavy hydrogen, but of course started the work much earlier. Heavy water was a key to nuclear reactors that produced U^{235} and plutonium as well as power.

Executive Privilege

In 1934, I worked at the Agricultural Adjustment Administration where Alger Hiss was Associate General Counsel and directly for him on loan to the Senate Munitions Committee. For the Committee, I wrote a paper on Executive

Privilege and concluded that there was such a privilege. I do not now recall whether the charges later made against Hiss included passing on atomic secrets. Probably not. Of course, his conviction was for perjury, not alleged espionage, but occasion for the perjury was alleged to be assistance to the Russians.   I later learned that when a security check was made on me, Alger said he hardly knew me, 'he sends me copies of his articles from time to time', for which I am very grateful. He must have known that association with him was not helpful. [You were not supposed to see your own security check—this was before Freedom of Information—but as acting head of the Office of Alien Property, I did see mine.]   On Executive Privilege, my friend Raoul Berger (with his mysterious timing—just before Watergate) wrote a book concluding that there was none.

Government secrecy

About 1970, the Senate Committee on Government Operations, heir to McCarthy's Committee, demanded from OEO certain documents. I was unwilling to give them over unless I first deleted certain identifying details that would probably have gotten a man killed by a Chicago gang. I never refused. I repeatedly offered to give them the documents with suitable excisions and assured them that I *knew* that the Committee did not want the unexpurgated documents. The committee staff, the Committee leading members and finally the full Committee insisted, yes, they did. After pushing me hard and unsuccessfully but with curious expressions of admiration for my resourcefulness ("If you ever run for office, I'll vote for you" said Committee Counsel), the Committee complained to the White House. Nixon, on taking office had said he would cooperate with Congress and never withhold information.

I was called to the White House and met with Egil Krogh,

who directed me in the name of the President to turn over the papers. "This Administration will never claim Executive Privilege. I speak for the President when I say this." I replied and I pray there is a tape of this (I am sure the Senate Committee had rather clumsily taped me—there was always a half-open desk drawer near my chair): "You are making a mistake. The day will come when you will want to claim Executive Privilege and when you do, you will be in a much better position if, instead of having said, this Administration will never claim the privilege, you have said that you will claim it only reluctantly and in a discriminating manner. Then, when you do claim it, you will be more likely to be sustained."

I went back to OEO under orders to deliver the papers and reported to the Director (Harding) that I had such orders and would not comply. He said that he would "back me up". What could that mean? It could mean that he would get fired, but he couldn't stop them from firing me or smearing me. So I turned over the papers after making the deletions I had wanted to make and flagging the fact that I had done so. The Committee, having won on paper a victory of principle, never complained but did leak the contents, as I had expected, to a newsman friendly to them (Clark Mollenhoff).

On Executive Privilege, in U.S. v. Nixon, a unanimous Supreme Court including, I think four of Nixon's own appointees, held that there is Executive Privilege, but that Nixon's claim of it (to protect his tapes) was not justified (July 1974). This precipitated Nixon's resignation (August 1974).

I can time my visit to Egil Krogh, because while I was with him, I heard him tell the Secretary of the Interior, Walter Hickel, very condescendingly, that the President was very busy and he didn't know that he could get the Secretary an appointment with the President. Hickel resigned in 1971. (The Watergate break-in was in June 1972. Nixon resigned in August 1974. I moved from OEO to HEW in 1973.)

Mike

Michael was born April 3, 1945. The first A-bomb dropped in anger was at Hiroshima, August 6, 1945. Mike was at Raquette in a crib and I was there on one of my more or less weekly trips. On the way up, I heard an announcement that Truman would speak that evening. I parked my car near the dining room and heard Truman on my car radio because it was more reliable than the others at camp. I heard Harry Truman announce the first use of the power of the atom. I was not at first fully convinced that he meant it literally. He could have been using hyperbole for simply an unusually powerful chemical bomb. But a darkness exploded before my closed eyes and I asked myself in terror (as many others did) what life is left for the new generation we are bringing forth. This has hung over my life since. I have often wondered how much Mike's life and Jan's was unsettled by being born when the fruit of that forbidden tree brought death into the world and destroyed our confidence of survival.

How

As early as August 1945, the Army made publicly available a detailed report on how the bomb works and the history of its development. This was signed by H.D. Smyth who was one of the principal workers on the bomb project. It was, I understand, ghost written by the great physicist Feynman. It withholds certain information for security reasons, of course, but it is remarkable in the openness of what it does tell. The original edition was a lithoprint, but in September it was put out by Princeton University Press as a well-printed paperback with some additions. Among other things it gives some support, without absolutely confirming it, to the story of my father's uranium ore analysis being as he thought the first. Describing the situation some 40 years later than Pop's analysis, p.36, "up to 1940 the total amount of uranium metal produced in this country was not more than a few grams and even this was of doubtful purity . . ." (p.40) "little or no uranium metal had been produced up to 1940 and *information was so scant that even the melting point was not known.*" (p.92) "At the end of 1941 the only uranium metal in existence was a few grains of good material ... and a few pounds of highly impure pyrophoric powder ... the only considerable amount ... was in the form of a commercial grade of black uranium oxide ... [which] contained 2 to 5 percent of impurities ... "

I sent for the report, read it. How is this a connection that links me in any personal sense to the bomb? If you enroll as connections everyone who has read about the bomb, the whole literate world is counted. What is significant, if anything, is that I reached out for the first available explanation. I had sufficient interest to read carefully the fairly high-level exposition, to savor the connections of ideas, the manner of exposition. Although I never fully mastered the substance, I retained enough for it to become part of work I did later. This is the usual style of my character and growth. It makes me, I think, a good generalist but master of no trade. In several areas, symbolic logic for one, I have been creative at a second level, but never at a first level. My work in symbolic logic and in the application of symbolic logic to law may be superior to that of say, most of what has been published in Jurimetrics, but I have read Willard Van Orman Quine. I admire Willard Quine—*And, Malcolm, you are no Willard Quine.*

Alamogordo

My friend Marvin Goidell, Captain in the Engineers Corps (later Major) was in charge of buying real estate for (among other purposes) the bomb building and testing project. Marvin was a friend of Irma's brother Bud, a fraternity brother. Then he became a close friend of Irma's and mine, of Pop's, of Gabe's and George's, of David's, and particularly of Irv's and Helen's. He considered himself an honorary Mason.

At first, Marvin did not know what the real estate was being used for. About this, two stories. In charge of the bomb project was Maj. Gen. L.R. Groves.

Marvin's first encounter with General Groves was a phone call directing him to acquire real estate described by metes and bounds. Marvin said,—General, as you speak I have roughly plotted out what you are saying. That is about half the State of Nevada. [Perhaps an exaggeration. I would guess it was more like 2500 square miles.]—I know that, Captain.—General, what is the purpose of this acquisition?—Captain, that is not your business. Buy it, that's an order.—I'm sorry, General, but for an acquisition of this magnitude, I will have to have a written request with a statement of purpose. General Groves slammed down the phone. Fifteen minutes later, a phone call from the Secretary of War (Stimson?).—Captain Goidell, I understand that General Groves has asked you to make a somewhat unusual acquisition.—Yes, Mr. Secretary.—Captain, I would appreciate it as a *personal* favor if you would do whatever the General asks and ask no questions.—Yes, Mr. Secretary.—Thank you, Captain.

Oak Ridge

Another story. Later, Marvin got to know General Groves very well and they were on good terms, but Marvin still did not know why they were buying all this property. On a long trip to inspect some site, Marvin said, General, you know I have the highest security clearances. It would help me to do my job better if you would tell me what the purpose of what we are doing is. Groves:—Marvin, you are right, I think it is time I told you: We are building plants to attach the back half of horses to the front half.

Saratoga

For several summers in the '40's and '50's, I drove to Raquette Lake from Washington or New York. Near Saratoga, the road passed a large stretch of land with no visible explanation of purpose. It had barbed wire, no-trespassing signs, and a deep screen of heavily planted pine trees behind which, what? I later learned this was an atomic bomb research center managed by General Electric.

Coffee

When I went to Brussels from Paris in 1947 for Inter-Custodial negotiations, the train served coffee made of acorns. The waiter counseled us not to order it but to wait. *Once the train crossed the border into Belgium, the same dining car served real coffee* (like an American train serving liquor only in wet states, not in dry states). *The reason was: the Belgian Congo had Uranium and Belgium was therefore rich.* For the same reason, at the Festival of Binche (Winter—Feb., Mar.? 1947, celebrating the discovery and occupation of America when Belgium had a Spanish princess), Belgians could gleefully throw oranges at each other in the streets. My English colleagues, for whom in their time of austerity, oranges were yearned for but beyond reach, looked on, horrified, but finally joined in the madness. Shortly before, Winston Churchill, at a sumptuous dinner in his honor in Brussels, had said: "Next time, *you* liberate *us*."

Heavy Water

My friend, Erik Poulsson, whom I met in Brussels in 1947, had been head of Intelligence for the Norwegian Underground during the German Occupation. He was probably involved in withholding heavy water from the Germans that they needed for their research on the bomb. I don't know that he was, but the circumstances suggest it. He was writing an autobiography but I don't know whether it was ever finished or published; if it had been, I think he would have told me. I am thinking of two episodes, primarily. Erik was attorney for Norsk Hydro and a Director when I knew him and I believe before the war. Norsk Hydro was a major producer of heavy water. Norwegian snow is particularly rich in heavy water and Norsk Hydro had the electric power to separate it from normal water sources. English commandos with help from the Norwegian Underground raided and destroyed Norsk Hydro's heavy water plant in the mountains (northwest of Oslo?). The other incident: A ferry taking

(Norwegian?) heavy water south from Norway?, Denmark?, Sweden?, to Germany (or to Denmark and thus to Germany) was sunk by the Underground along with innocent passengers whose lives were knowingly sacrificed to keep the secret of the plans to sink the ship.

OSS

Helen Hornstein came to Washington in the 1940's as part of the flood of 'girls' who came then. She shared an apartment on Wisconsin Avenue across from the Cathedral and worked for a predecessor to the OSS, predecessor to the CIA, as secretary to one of the principal managers. I don't know, really know, what, if any, relation OSS had to the bomb, but I assume it was part of its mission to learn what progress the Germans were making in developing a bomb, where, who, and to identify researchers that could be useful and rescue them perhaps in Denmark or elsewhere. Helen assisted Max Lowenthal on a White House visit. She was told to ask whether he could see the President that afternoon. She thought that was absurd but dutifully called. The President's scheduler asked, will 1:30 be all right? Lowenthal said yes. She waited outside in a taxi but then took notes of his hasty and half-heard report dictated in a soft voice through the traffic din in a taxi with open windows (no air-conditioning). Lowenthal was pleased with her reconstruction and invited her to come to Berlin where he was going as Advisor to General Clay. She accepted, thinking it was a joke, but she promptly got travel orders and went. When she got there she found Lowenthal wasn't coming after all, but Irwin Mason, then at the Embassy in Paris was coming instead. She didn't like the change, didn't like the sound of him when he called her from Paris and said he was coming, didn't like the sound or sight of him when he arrived. I went to Berlin in 1947 in defiance of orders from Washington. I was in Brussels and was damned if I would go home as directed without seeing my brother. A Canadian Colonel wrote travel orders for himself and for me. I saw Irv, and as I was leaving met an assistant to my brother (Helen) at the Railroad Station without knowing who she was or even catching her name. Knowing it was a long trip and the train had no dining car, she had brought me a lunch box. Reader, she married him (1948). ("Mally knows the girl.") When my mother asked me about her, I could tell her nothing (what are you hiding?).

6/26/93

Hiroshima

At dinner at Pat and Fielding O.s, Grace and I met Bob and Ruth Loevinger who are old friends of the O.s and, until recently, neighbors.

Bob Loevinger had worked for Eastman Kodak (in Chicago and in Los Angeles?) developing cinefilm. He got his doctorate in physics (specializing in radiation measurement?), worked as a medical physicist at Mount Sinai (I assumed in New York, but there is also a Mount Sinai in Chicago). Then he was at Los Alamos and later at the Bureau of Standards and Technology. At Los Alamos, he took movies of the test explosion in Nevada. (I don't know whether that was officially or unofficially, he didn't say.)

When the bomb was dropped at Hiroshima, cinefilm was made by an automatic camera in the plane and sent then to California (Los Angeles?). Loevinger, presumably because of his expertise in developing cinefilm, was sent to Los Angeles, where the Army was instructed to give him anything he needed. Kodak Laboratories were instructed to turn over developing facilities to him, but without any knowledge of what he would be developing. He first ran the equipment to make sure that it was in good working order so that the film would not be injured. Then he developed the bomb film (which later, I believe, was widely disseminated for propaganda and educational purposes). He brought the film back to Los Alamos. Because Groves and

Oppenheimer were not on good terms, Oppenheimer was afraid that Groves might hijack the film. Loevinger's instructions were not to surrender the film to anyone, not even to General Groves, unless a gun was pointed at him. In that case, he was to give them up. Groves did not hijack them.

Ruth Loevinger is a Rockville social worker. She is a member of Grace's Monday book club.

Bob Loevinger is a younger brother (by three years) of Lee Loevinger, Minnesota lawyer, former Commissioner of the FCC. Lee was a leading promoter of Jurimetrics magazine, which published my article on the Logical Structure of a Proposition of Law. Before my article was published it was sent to an anonymous peer reviewer who recommended publication. I have assumed that the anonymous reviewer was Lee Loevinger How many symbolic logicians are there who are lawyers?

10/12/95

In our group of 31 Elderhostlers (Sept. 1995), two had some role that I learned related to the A-bomb. Dorothy R. teaches mathematics at Hunter? She studied under Koopman, under whom I studied fairly elementary calculus. Koopman was a great mathematician and was involved in work on the bomb. Dorothy says that, as a graduate student, she was assigned to do calculations of which she did not know the purpose (others, as well, got similar assignments). She later learned that they related to the bomb.

Leo H. is a professor of chemical engineering at Auburn University, Auburn, Alabama. He says he worked at Oak Ridge, Tennessee and made an invention that was patented. [If an invention is made using an employer's resources, the employer may have a right to an assignment—"shop right". I don't know whether that is automatic or has to be stipulated in the employment contract]. Leo says most employers give you $1 for the assignment because there has to be a payment, but Oak Ridge gave him $10.

Irwin's Party

Nat and Griselda Lobell were both at Columbia Law School about when I was there as a faculty assistant and Irma and my brother Irv were students. They were good friends of all of us.

Nat was a talented painter, potter, etcher, fiddler, and builder of violas. He was also a talented lawyer. He worked for the SEC as, I believe, Executive Assistant to the Commission. Griselda worked for Felix Cohen's study of the law of American Indians. When America entered the War, the SEC moved to Philadelphia. Griselda has written me some stories and has authorized me to re-tell them.

Lucy Kramer (Cohen) came to Philadelphia to visit Victoria Weiss and introduced Nat to Paul Weiss (who was Chairman of the Philosophy Department at Bryn Mawr). Griselda had one baby and soon had a second. She found a comfortable coterie of women with babies, many of them teachers. My brother Irv said he was coming to visit them on a certain weekend. Griselda decided it was time for a party. She invited her women friends and their husbands and some of Nat's colleagues and their wives, bought records for square dancing and drilled Nat in calling the dances. Victoria Weiss said she had a friend, a French woman in Princeton. Griselda said, Bring her. Nat said this party will never gel.

Irv didn't show. The French woman called afterwards to say she had been in America several years, but this was the first time she had met "real Americans". When the bomb was dropped at Hiroshima, it turned out the French woman had been working on the bomb and she now could go home and work on the bomb and nuclear power for France, where she was now able to live (she was Jewish). [Irv showed up a week after this party. Where were you when we ran a party in your honor? Irv smiled and said nothing.]

SEC staff dinner

Shortly after their second baby was born, the Lobells were invited to a dinner of the SEC staff at a downtown hotel (1944). Griselda found none of her dresses would fit above the waist. She put on, instead, a blue suit. The jacket would fit if she didn't button it. She wore a white blouse, a string of pearls, and pearl earrings. Her hair was a mess so she put on a blue beret, combed her hair forward and cut it in light brown bangs. She hoped they would sit in an inconspicuous corner but it did not turn out that way. At the hotel they were joined by Florence and Mort Yohalem. Then the Chairman's Secretary, who had organized the party, and Commissioner Pike. Then Abner G. and Lou & Bernice Loss. Pike sat next to Griselda. At the dinner, he first made general conversation as politeness required, but then focused on Griselda. He told her that after living in New York City, he had gone to Africa where he made a good deal of money in the diamond trade and described his life there. He had then gone back to Wall Street. Then, feeling that he should give something to public service, he had gone to the Commission. He also told her of the cranberry bogs his family owned on Cape Cod and of the joy with which every year, at the appropriate time, family members from all over would gather, put on boots, and pick cranberries.

As a Commissioner, Pike was often absent from meetings, called to Washington. On such occasions he would brief Nat on his views on the issues that would be taken up and when he returned, Nat would report to him what had happened.

After the night of the dinner, when he met with Nat, he was very solicitous about asking about Griselda's health. Nat said, I must get to the bottom of this, but it took a while.

When Pike lived in New York City, he was engaged. He and his fiancée went to the Beaux-Arts Ball. They had a very pleasant time. His fiancée was dressed in a blue suit, white blouse, string of pearls, pearl earrings, a blue beret, light brown hair in bangs. At the end of the party, she returned her ring and said she was eloping that night with another man. She had not wanted to spoil the party by telling him sooner. Pike never married.

In Pike's strange preoccupation with Griselda at the SEC staff dinner, he had, evidently, been telling his former fiancée, through Griselda, what he had done since then.

When the bomb dropped at Hiroshima, Pike left the SEC to join the Atomic Energy Commission, thus explaining his frequent mysterious trips to Washington.

OAP

The Office of Alien Property, of which I was General Counsel 1948-1950, and for periods acting head, controlled any German intellectual property in the United States and some of that seized abroad. We had a part in sponsoring the (Goudsmit?) mission that was sent to learn how close Germany had come to the bomb and to screen the German scientists involved—a job badly done I understand because of the non-cooperation of the State and Defense Departments.

AEP

About 1948, Donald Cook was briefly Alien Property Custodian. He had been at SEC, went into private practice with Raoul Berger. Was later Chairman of the SEC. He then became President of American Electric Power, which distinctively urged the benefits of atomic power and coal power over oil power. Perhaps about 1970, I had money to invest and bought AEP stock because I had confidence in Don Cook's eye for the main chance, but discovered that Don Cook was no longer there (had died?).

Shelter

In the '40's and '50's there was a strong emphasis on establishing shelter from nuclear attack. School children were drilled in how to take shelter in case of attack. So far as I know, the Steiner School did not put a strong emphasis on this, but they must have complied, for it was legally required. Nationally there was a strong emphasis on building shelters, covering your face in the event of attack and so on. Irma and I were concerned about the balance between some marginal protection for the children, and the harm of having them grow up in so explicitly unfriendly a world. We did not really believe that the shelter program would save lives, and felt that it was basically propaganda to get across the idea that Russia was wicked (which it was but this was a poor way to teach it).

ER

About 1955-1966, I was active in the Democratic Reform Movement in New York. Many in the movement were anti-nuclear bomb and anti-nuclear power. (I did not agree with then on this and for many of them had little personal respect.) Eleanor Roosevelt was an icon and active member of this movement in the Democratic Party. (She had, it seemed to me, a tendency to align herself with the establishment side of the movement—perhaps good politics but disappointing.) Franklin Roosevelt authorized the Manhattan Project. I have no knowledge that Mrs. Roosevelt had any significant connection with the Project, but I intend to check this a little further.

Mid-Continent

About 1960, I was a director of Mid-Continent Uranium Corporation (Colorado). It was, I believe, the only American uranium corporation that was profitable. I was nominated by my client, Ralph De Pasquale, who controlled a substantial block of stock. Another block was held by a former governor (or current governor?) of Colorado and his friends. There was a proxy fight and Ralph was forced out with, I think, the active connivance of the SEC Regional Office which, improperly in my opinion, gave color to a circulated story that De Pasquale was involved in a stock fraud. While I was a Director, I visited the mines, donning protective gear and a telltale sensitive label and crawling through narrow passages in the rock.

City Bar

About 1962, I was a member of the Atomic Energy Law Committee of the Bar Association of the City of New York, as liaison member for the Administrative Law Committee. Not surprisingly, the Committee was clearly weighted toward atomic power and had a close association with the Atomic Forum, which seemed to be a trade association of the industry. (Although I agreed with their stand as a whole, I thought the Committee should have had a better balance.) Among other topics, we studied responsibility of nuclear plants for catastrophic accidents ["Price-Anderson insurance", e.g., referred to in my article, On teaching legal history backwards, 18 Jour. Leg. Ed., No. 2, 155 (1966), and handling spent fuel, still a problem].

AEC

About 1965, I wrote a paper on the deficiencies of the Atomic Energy Commission. This was requested by The Scientists' Committee on Public Policy (exact name?). It was submitted, peer reviewed, and approved. It was intended for publication in a Symposium on atomic power: methods, economics, dangers, problems, legal aspects, future. The Symposium was never published because many of the other contributions took so long to be delivered that parts of the book became outdated before the book was completed. Too bad. It was a good paper and might have led me into other directions.

SALT

1973-1975, I was Special Counsel to John B. Rhinelander, General Counsel, HEW. He had been Legal Advisor to the SALT I Delegation, Washington 1971-1972 (and Iceland at the time the new island erupted). Later he was active in Bar Association and other work related to arms limitations.

1972, I went to Russia with Ken Adelman and others. He and I were repeatedly thrown out of Patrice Lumumba University, but he persisted and succeeded in staying overnight, proving that he knew how to deal with the Russians. (I quit because Irma was not well, in the hotel alone, and we were leaving very early the next morning.) He was then Special Assistant to VISTA, later Director of Arms Control and Disarmament Agency 1983 to about 1989.

Of course, since I worked in Washington so long, I naturally knew many people who could be counted as connections to the bomb. I mention only a few that pop into my head.

Space

My friend and co-author, Paul Dembling, was General Counsel of the National Air and Space Administration and of its predecessor, National Advisory Committee on Aeronautics (1952-1958, 1958-1969), and of the General Accounting Office (GAO) (1969-1978), and President, U.S. International Institute for Space Law.

The Hard Way to Peace

Amitai Etzioni, an Israeli War of Independence hero, a yekke (that is an Israeli of German origin, the kind that wears a jacket and maybe even a tie). He came to the United States where he has become well known as a sociologist at Columbia and then at George Washington University. In the 1960's, he gave several lectures on a gradualist approach to arms reduction, which, contrary to usual approaches, disarms conventional arms first while retaining nuclear arms. The nuclear arms, it is hoped, are less likely to be used, but stand as a guarantor against violators of the conventional arms reductions agreements until both sides become convinced that nuclear reductions are feasible. Irma and Serah Scheinman and I went to hear him. *Irma and I then helped Bob Clampitt arrange a series of seminars on nuclear arms and nuclear power, based in part on Etzioni's book, The Hard Way to Peace* [1962], with very well informed speakers brought in from Washington, and others. Mostly West Siders attended.

FBA—Committee on Frederal Grants

At Paul Dembling's suggestion, I created for the Federal Bar Association a Committee on Federal Grants (about 1978). *As a major undertaking of the Committee, I drafted and the Committee approved an Outline on the Use of Grants in the Energy Field.*

My standards of inclusion in this listing have been very lax. I have simply let the central topic of atomic weapons and atomic power stimulate recollections and associations. Many things included have a thin connection. Many other connections are not mentioned. Some of these associations, however, do connect me with the topic even though, like Mar Ploni (Hebrew Mr. Anonymous, Mr. Somebody-or-other) I have made no contribution either to furthering or slowing the development of atomic power and weapons. The connections exist because I live in my century. They are part of my Abominable Autobiography.

Irma's line

8/4/91

Irma's father was Samuel Herman Slosberg. He manufactured or sold ladies collars and cuffs, resembling in this the Mosesson-Ritevsky galanterie business. He married Anne Binder and they had three children spaced three years apart; 1910, 1913, 1916, Irma, Bud, Bob. In my family, we were also steps, 5 years part, Bryna, Malcolm, Irv, 1905, 1910, 1915. I believe there is some parallelism in our personalities: Bryna—Irma, Malcolm—Bud, Irv—Bob—not absolute, but significant.   Sam's father was Ira, for whom Irma was named.   Sam and Anne then divorced bitterly, about 1917. Irma retained the bitterness of the divorce. Bud however, kept some kind of connection, and I met Sam at Bud's graduation from Law School. He seemed pleasant. We had not told him of our marriage nor did we tell him later of the birth of our children. I believe he remarried and had new children.

Irma's grandfather on her mother's side was Jehiel (Jacob) Binder. His grandfather was Rabbi Jehiel Heller. He was descended from Rabbi Yom Tob Lippman Heller, who was descended from Rabbis of the 11th Century, Nathan and Yehiel of Rome.

Rabbi Jehiel Heller (1814-1861) had a daughter (1846-1876). In 1860 she married Ben Zion Binder. They had a son Jehiel (Jacob) Binder (1861-1920). He had six siblings. I have their birth years according to Anne Binder Slosberg, but not their names. Jehiel (Jacob) Binder was a prominent builder in New York. Bud recalled being driven about town by an uncle who pointed out buildings that Jacob Binder had put up. These were primarily in Brooklyn, but some in the Bronx and some in Manhattan between 150th and 160th Streets. Possibly Binder knew my grandfather Abe Kahn who was also a builder in New York. Because of a credit crunch, Binder's partners went bankrupt but he insisted on paying his creditors in full. His reputation meant everything to him.

Ben Zion, in a second marriage, married Nechama, in her third marriage. Nechama died about 1900. I do not have her last name. Her first name means comfort and may possibly mean that she was posthumous. She married Becker and had a child Hinde (1867-1911). Nechama's second marriage was to Noodelman who changed his name to Needleman. They had a son Notte (Nathan) Nadelman and a daughter Chayeraisel. Nechama then married Ben Zion Binder about 1880. They had two daughters, Channe who married Max Chiger, and Elkahanna, who married Shapiro. Channe and Max Chiger had Ben (b. 1902), Sam (b. 1904), Betty (b. 1910) and Artie (called Archie, b. 1913). Betty was about the same age as Irma. Archie was about the same age as Bud. I have met some of the Chigers at family parties and funerals and got some family stories from them.

After Nechama married Ben Zion, her oldest daughter Hinde Becker became part of the Binder family group, but was not related to them by blood. She and Jacob Binder fell in love and eloped. They had five children: Max (b. 1890), Anne Harriet (b. 1892), Irving (b. 1895), Sim Chat (b. 1897), and Nancy May (b. 1902). Hinde died (about 1911) of leukemia.

I have pictures of Jacob (Jehiel) and have or had pictures of Hinde. From the photos, Jan drew portraits which she gave to Anne. We don't know what happened to them when Anne died. If possible, I'll include them.

(Helen Woltman): On weekends (Friday afternoons?) Jacob Binder would bring home a huge slab of chocolate for the family. When they cut up the chocolate bar to distribute it, Sim would bring out a scale to be sure every piece was equal and that he got a fair share.

Jacob was not religious. Hinde kept a kosher house and lit candles. She would not let them eat out—she would make what they ate.

Jacob had a carriage and two horses, kept at a stable a few blocks away. Hinde was a "dresser" with robes, laces, jewels. There were full length painted portraits of Jacob and of Hinde in her robes and jewels. They were in the living room, but Helen does not know what became of them. After Hinde died, Jacob married again but the marriage did not last. The new wife perhaps got rid of the portraits.

Jacob was crazy about Irma. He got up at 5AM and took Irma out at 6AM in her baby carriage to sit in the park. Jacob got fur collars and fur beret for Nan and he had small sizes made for Irma.

Max married Anna, a nurse, who had died (about 1931) by the time I knew the family. His father put him in a hat business. He gambled it away. His father threw him out. He was a talented musician, played any instrument, fiddle, woodwinds, brass, piano, accordion. For a while he traveled with Anna on cruise ships: she was the ship's nurse, he and his combo entertained. He was always traveling with a combo. It was later said that he never paid board. Wherever his combo traveled, there was always a landlady glad to have him. I met him only once, at Anne's apartment in the Oliver Cromwell (West 72nd Street near Central Park). I don't remember, but he may have come for Irma's and my marriage; it was about that time (1935). Max, it is said, had no love for his sister Anne.

Irving married Shirley. At one time, when we lived on West End Avenue(1950-1966), they lived near us on Columbus Avenue? and came to visit us. He was an engineer, specializing in heating and ventilation. In those days, Jews were not welcome as engineers. He may have chosen that career because his father was a prominent builder.

Irving Binder was a long distance runner. He won medals. Sim was his trainer. Irv ran with a Swedish Athletic Club in Brooklyn. The newspapers wrote him up as Irving Binder the Swede.

Sim Chat married Florence Rutchik. Sim had reluctantly gone to engineering school to please his father. When his father died (1920), he said he really wanted to be a lawyer. His brother Irv agreed to support him through law school, but he almost did not become a lawyer. The family had a summer place on the Long Island Sound. Irma came by train. Sim met the train. As Irma went on ahead, Sim picked up two bags that he thought were hers. A woman screamed Stop thief and insisted on having him arrested. With some difficulty, he finally persuaded the district attorney and later the Bar character committee that it was an innocent mistake.

Sim organized the Diamond Club in New York. During World War II, he did Foreign Funds work, perhaps because of the Belgian Jews in the diamond trade. Irma ghostwrote for him an article on Foreign Funds because his name on the article would have more practical consequence than hers. He also represented the Belgian writer, Sim or Simenon. I admired Simenon and hoped to meet him through Sim Binder, but did not. Sim had heart trouble and was put on a strict rice diet by Duke University. Sim and Florence had a daughter, Jane, no doubt named for Jehiel (Jacob). She married twice, first Howard Dubin, then Dana Binkhoff. In her first marriage she had two daughters, Sue and Jill Ellen. Jane now [1991] has four grandchildren. Her older daughter, Sue, has two daughters and the younger daughter, Jill Ellen, who is an engineer, has two children(a boy and, I think, a girl). Jill Ellen and her husband, who is also an engineer, built their own house in Pennsylvania. When Jane wanted to be admitted to Radcliffe, I asked Harvard Professor Stanley Surrey to put in a good word for her. He replied that, since he didn't know her but knew me, he wrote to praise me, saying I recommended her, so the outcome *might* be that *I* would be admitted to Radcliffe. (It didn't work out that way.) I believe Jane was admitted to Radcliffe but chose to go to Cornell where she got a good scholarship.

Nancy May (b. 1902) was probably named for Nechama (who died about 1900). She was only 8 years older than Irma, and they were particularly close, although, Anne and Nancy May had some family squabbles. Nancy married Louis Woltman. He was a clothing salesman. He was of Romanian stock and came to America in 1913 by way of England (perhaps because of the Kishinev pogroms in 1903). He spoke with a strong English accent, which was advantageous in a clothing business. The first suit I bought was a pepper and salt gray that cost $30 and lasted 20 years and was still entirely good but my waist line had outgrown it. Each customer had a page in his notebook but he didn't need it because he remembered their sizes of suits, shirts, underwear, socks. Often, wives and mothers would order clothes from him without their men because they trusted his taste and judgment. When I moved to Washington and could not get clothing from him I asked Bud to go shopping with me and when Bud could not go I asked Irma to go.

They had a daughter, Helen Lee, and a son, Joel Dan. Joel married first Stephanie Pollikoff and second Joan Wilkie. They have a son Eric Scott who is very attractive. Helen Lee was named for Hinde Becker, but her name Lee comes from the name of a movie star of whom Irma was very fond. Helen has been a law secretary and law office manager and a fund-raiser for Jewish charities. She was a very pretty child. She and her friend Michael have traveled together, particularly to Hong Kong where they have friends whose son is their god-son. Michael has a striking resemblance to Albert Einstein. Once when they visited

Washington, I took them to see the statue of Einstein at the National Science Foundation. Other visitors gasped and asked Michael to pose for pictures with Albert.

Sim was early warned of his dangerous high blood pressure. Nan was always known as "delicate". Don't upset Nan, she is not feeling well. She died just short of her 95th birthday.

Sim looked so strong but went so soon (in his mid 50s).

Helen has blue eyes but changeable—sometimes hazel, sometimes she says grey. Nan had brown eyes but Jacob Binder had blue eyes and Lou Woltman very blue eyes. Eric also, I think. Irma's eyes were also changeable, but typically hazel.

Anne married Sam Slosberg. Their first child was Irma (1910-1985). She married me in 1934 in a civil wedding and again in a religious wedding in 1935, performed to satisfy my mother. The wedding was performed at Anne's apartment by Rabbi Solomon, a very flexible Mason Family rabbi. He asked whether we wanted the service to be Orthodox or Reform, long or short. We elected Reform and short. We then had dinner downstairs in the Oliver Cromwell dining room. Among the Slosberg guests were Judge Panken who spoke, telling a Yiddish Hitler story, his daughter Hermione (a friend of Irma's), John Slawson, head of the Jewish Board of Guardians. We have two children, Mike (b. 1945) and Jan (b. 1946). Jan married Edward T. Freundschuh. They have two children, Sharan Raedriel (b. 1984) and Amber Grace (b. 1986). Irma taught at a school in Queens. The school was a special school with a tradition going back before it became part of the New York school system (Newton High School). After we met, Irma wanted to teach in Manhattan. She went to visit a family friend in the Board of Education who said, if you can teach shorthand I can get you what you want. Irma said sure.

Over the summer she studied Gregg, and I drilled her. She passed a test and got a job (in a night school?) in mid-West Side.

We thought it would be a good idea for Irma to go to Law School, but the Columbia Dean decided that her degree of B.S. (Drexel) did not make her eligible. I told her that New York then permitted Bar admission based on studying with a lawyer and she could do that with me. Instead, Irma then wrote her first and successful brief in which she proved that she had as many hours of humanities (Shakespeare, Picaresque novels and so on) many of them at the University of Pennsylvania, as she would have had, had she obtained a B.A. at Barnard.

Her first class (to which she must have come late) was criminal law. She came home and asked what was all the talk of men's rear? This was mens rea (law latin for guilty mind).

I was a faculty assistant at the time. The faculty all knew we were married but Irma did not want to trade on our connection, so she registered as Miss Slosberg. Professor Handler came rushing into class one day, posed the question of the day (like Professor Goebel, he would then spend the hour asking a student variations of the question). He called on Mrs. Mason. Irma gave no sign that she had heard him. Again he called, Mrs. Mason. She looked right at him and did not acknowledge him. He looked, flustered, at his seating chart, couldn't find any Mrs. Mason, and hastily called Mr. Jones.

I was technically on the staff of the Puerto Rican Reconstruction Finance Corporation and expected to report there. What would Irma do? She went to her professors and asked whether she could get credit for doing research in Puerto Rican law. Several professors agreed—research in condominium law—then standard in Puerto Rico but hardly known here—now standard here too; research in Puerto Rican Administrative Law. The Dean said, Columbia is not a correspondence school. She talked him into giving her credit for the work and she registered. But then I didn't go to Puerto Rico. Well, she talked him into giving her tuition back.

We moved to Washington and Irma switched to George Washington where she got her degree. She passed the DC. Bar and started practice there. I was not admitted in DC. Irma was not admitted in New York, but she could be my assistant in New York and I could be her assistant in DC.

When Irma became quite ill with asthma, allergies and emphysema, she entertained herself watching Star Trek and reading at least one mystery story a day.

Jan recalls that she had watched the first run of Star Trek, Irma watched a rerun and she and Jan would discuss the shows together.

I used to get a constant flow of mystery stories from the Bethesda Branch Library, often five or six at a time. Soon the librarians knew me and knew Irma's taste. They would tell me she will like that, or she won't like that but we have put aside for you a mystery she will like. When Irma died, the librarians sent me a condolence note. I never go past the Library without remembering that.

Carolyn Kennedy married a Schlossberg. Of course, Slosberg = Sliosberg = Schlossberg. Nan says that the Slosberg name was formerly Schlossberg and Anne changed it to Slosberg.

In the 1930s, Anne went to a party at Ira Gershwin's. George was there and played the piano most of the evening. (I have an impression that Ira lived in the Oliver Cromwell as Anne did.) Anne came back thoroughly drunk. She stretched out on a couch in the living room declaring, My mind is crystal clear. (This became a family tease.)

Anne was Court Representative in the Juvenile Court for the Jewish Board of Guardians. She had grown up not speaking Yiddish, but she needed it for her job, so she learned it. A Yiddish newspaper carried a profile of her which ran something like this: If your son talks fresh, does not go to school, do not tear him limb from limb like a herring. Call up quick Gramercy___-_ _ _ _ [Anne's office number].

After Anne and Sam divorced, she married Don Adolfo Kates. It was probably her brother Sim who introduced them. Adolfo was a wholesale distributor in Cuba of U.S. pharmaceuticals and manufacturer of some cosmetics and nail polish and accessories, and Honorary Consul of Belgium to Cuba. He had a son José of a previous marriage. José had married Miriam and they had two children, a girl and a boy. He had developed a business of advising American companies on avoiding embarrassing mistranslations into Spanish. For example, papaya is acceptable in Mexico but not in Cuba, where it has pornographic flavor and must be called fruta bomba.

One day, Don Adolfo took Irma to the Havana Yacht Club. (A thé dansant). A young man came over and asked Irma if she would dance with him. Don Adolfo very angrily bawled the man out. How do you dare to ask my daughter without first asking my permission? [I think Irma would have liked to dance. She enjoyed dancing and I did not dance.]

Adolfo, in this, was reflecting the macho culture of his society. While not objecting to Adolfo's behavior, Irma strongly objected to the macho principle underlying it. As a result we never travelled later together to any Latin-American country. We did travel together to Norway, the Netherlands, Belgium, several times to France, England, Austria. Once when I had to go Germany, Irma refused to set foot there, but perhaps ten years later, she did go. We have also travelled together to Israel, to Russia, Finland, to Australia and New Zealand. Strangely, some places I know we went to have not left visa stamps in her passports. Perhaps they used a different system.

Don Adolfo sought to have a very fatherly relationship with Anne's family. Their marriage broke up, however, about the time Fidel came in. José moved to Mexico, Miriam and the children moved to Long Island. Don Adolfo moved to Florida and then to Long Island. Anne moved to Mexico where she created a library and was honored for it (see pictures, supra), then to New York and then to Washington where she lived in the same building with Irma and me, but in a separate apartment.

When Anne died, we had a small memorial in our apartment. I said that Anne would help anyone who needed help. BUT she would help her way, not the way the person wanted to be helped. I believe the family agreed. I also said that Yiddish is a very prudish language. Anne had told me the only dirty jokes I knew in Yiddish. Some of the younger family members asked for samples, but I refused to tell them.

Her second child was Bud (Hilburt), b. 1913, named after Hinde Becker. He married Louise Proser (d. Aug. 1985). They had two children, Lynn Allison and William Jay who married Kathleen Lyons (m. Sept. 14, 1985). They have, I believe, two children. Bud and Louise divorced but remained on close terms. Bud then married Hortense, but they later divorced as well.

When Bud was perhaps 10 and his brother Bob perhaps 7, they attended the Stephen Wise Free Synagogue Sunday School which then was held at Carnegie Hall on 57th Street, the new facility at 68th Street not being built yet. Bud had money for charitable contributions and for carfare (5 cents each, each way). The teacher told them about the starving Armenian children and took up a collection. She then announced that she had $15.90. Can anyone give another 10 cents to make an even $16? So Bud gave the 10 cents he had for carfare and the two walked home from 57th to 159th.

When Bud was in college (Dickinson), he was in charge of his fraternity's meals. He didn't do the cooking, but planned the meals and bought the makings. Later he enjoyed very much having guests that he could cook for.

During the Battle of the Bulge, he was stationed in the Bulge area, as a warrant officer armed with only a side-arm against possible attack by tanks, machine guns, rifles. Probably before the battle, my brother (Red Cross Field Director) located him and went to visit him.

Anne's third child was Bob Bennet who married Rita _____, had a son, Steven, and a daughter Jan Marcia. Steven married _____ Chait, and had a son. Bob Bennet may have been named for Ben Zion.

Bob went to Dickinson which had been Bud's school. He bought a Border Collie puppy and smuggled him into his dorm, but he was caught and expelled. He came home, gave me the puppy and went back to school. I brought up the puppy as a francophone. He was very well trained except that he hated sounds like gunshots and disliked any man wearing a uniform—soldiers, policemen, letter carriers. This dislike apparently did not apply to Bud when Bud joined the Army, however.

In the 1940s, Irma's allergist said she had to give up either the dog or her husband. We opted for giving up the dog. Bud, perhaps on his visit to his mother before going overseas, took Nank to Havana. When I went down with Irma later, I retrained him in Spanish (saute became brinca for jump and so on). He lived a happy life but died in the end of wounds incurred in macho roaming.

Bob moved in the 1940s to Florida and I knew less about him after that. I understand that Rita and Bob had franchises for making photographs of night club guests and did very well at it.

I never knew Jacob Binder, but from his pictures, I judge him to have had a sort of Prussian personality which I would say Bud shared.

Bud had a hot temper. He was a man of principle. He was guided by principle. He was a man of honor. He respected his word. He was a man of responsibility. When he undertook something, he followed through personally from top to bottom.

Bud was always willing to help those who needed help, but resented it when his help met with ingratitude, as often happened. In his last years, Bud was not well and was lonely. I would often meet people to whom Bud had been extraordinarily helpful. How is Bud?—He's managing. But you know, he'd love to see you.—Yes, I'll have to call him. (And then they didn't.) I urged Bud not to deprive himself of company, but he was determined not to call his old friends for lunch or dinner if they didn't call him.

One day, I went to visit Bud. He was suffering. I called his doctor. The doctor was away for a weekend and I got a replacement, who did not offer to see him—just said, it's back pain, give him aspirin. I didn't think it was back pain and said, Doctor, I think he belongs in the hospital. Oh, said the doctor contemptuously, *you* are going to prescribe now? Monday we took Bud to his doctor who said—the hospital right away. We took Bud to Georgetown Hospital where he was immediately operated on for an aneurysm. When he woke he was convinced he was in an Army hospital in Germany. He was sure it had been arranged by his first wife's uncle and was amazed that we had gotten there so quickly. We said, Bud, you are in Georgetown Hospital on R Street in Washington. We came down Wisconsin and turned right on R and parked in their parking lot. Bud would not believe us for months.

For several years after that, Bud showed a special form of depression—he concentrated on planning his Will, asking each of his relatives what they wanted him to leave them, and writing it down. I could not persuade him to turn to a more useful activity. In fact, he never completed his Will.

Pictures of Irma's Family

Pictures of Irma and her family in Chapter I, Starting, Chapter II, Learning

p. 154 Irma and Mike

p. 155 Irma, Malcolm, Mike, Jan Anne, Morris, Rae, Mike, Jan

p. 156 Irma and Jan

p. 159 Irma

p. 160 Irma, Jan, Sharan – "Three Women"

p. 260 Irma's brother Bud, Warrant Officer, with my brother Irv, Red Cross Field Director met (in Luxembourg before the Battle of the Bulge?)

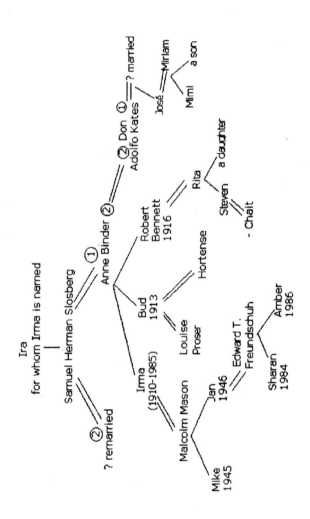

Irma's Father's Line

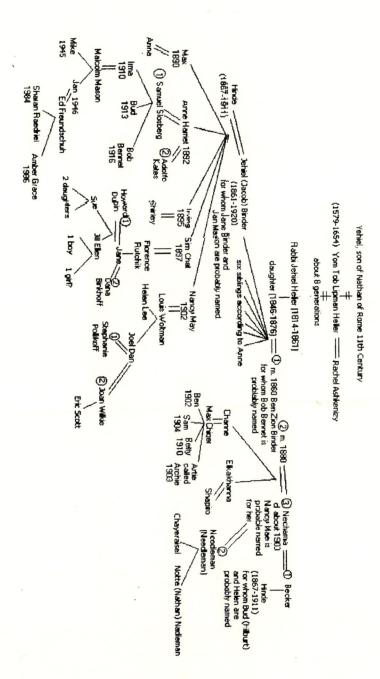

Irma's Mother's Line

Irma's grandfather, Jehiel (Jacob) Binder

Irma's grandfather, Jehiel (Jacob) Binder with Irma,
Bob Bennet, Bud about 1918

Max Binder

Irving Binder, January 3, 1926

Irma and Bud about 1915

Bob

Bud

Bob

Mal, Bud Slosberg, Bob Slosberg, Sam Slosberg
Irma and Anne
At Buds Graduation from Law School June 9, 1936

Bud in Havana?

Bud in Havana?

Don Adolfo and Irma

José Kates, Miriam, Anne,
Don Adolfo and Irma in Havana about 1947

José and Miriam Kates in Havana about 1947

Don Adolfo and Anne in Havana

Don Adolfo in Havana

Don Adolfo

Don Adolfo and Anne Kates

Mexico library party in honor of Irma's mother, Anne Kates

Mexico library party

Irma

Irma and Nank

Bud

Irma's Passport 1950

Irma's Passport 1955

Irma's Passport 1969

Irma's Passport 1976

Irma at Phillips Radio about 1951

Irma and Mal

Irma and Mal at Raquette

Jan 2 and Mike 3 at Raquette 1948

Mike 3 and Jan 2 at Raquette 1948

Irma with Mike and Jan at Raquette

Irma, Mal, and Jan at Raquette

Irma at Raquette

Kids climbing into the rafters at Raquette

Kids in the rafters at Raquette

Irma

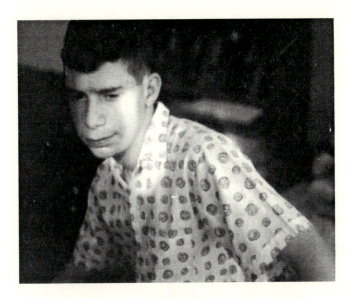

Mike

Hungry Mike

Jan in her teens

Jan holding a bouquet of radishes from her garden in
Star Hill, Arkansas

Russ Packard, Irma and Mal

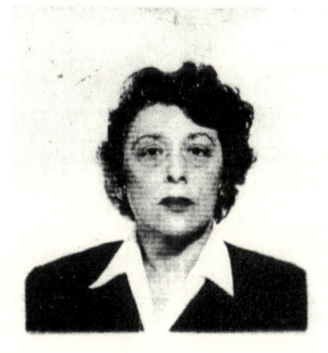

La Belle "Drug-Addict"

Irma

Irma

Irma

Irma and Malcolm

Irma

A tribute to Dr. Silver
Irma swimming in Bronz's pool one month after discharge from ICU in 1972.

Irma and Mal during Kagao visit

Irma and Mal

Eric Woltman in 1988, age 16

Anne Kates and Irma

Irma in Chevy Chase about 1985

Irma amidst the forsythia in Chevy Chase 1985

AAA – Agricultural Adjustment Administration

ABA – American Bar Association

AEC – Atomic Energy Commission

APC/OAP – Alien Property Custodian (Independent)/Office of Alien Property (Department of Justice)

DGAB – Departmental Grant Appeals Board

FCC – Federal Communications Commission

HEW – Department of Health, Education and Welfare

HHS – Department of Health and Human Services

NLRB – National Labor Relations Board

OEO – Office of Economic Opportunity

OMB – Office of Management and Budget

OSS – Office of Strategic Services

SALT – Strategic Arms Limitation Treaty

SEC – Securities and Exchange Commission

TMT – Tomorrow's Methods Today – a shipping company that went bankrupt because of the explosion of its principal ship, The Carib Queen.